How to teach the catechism to children

Mrs. Frank C. Horton

Covenant Presbytery

Published by
Covenant Presbytery's Christian Education Committee

Post Office Box 102, Carrollton, Mississippi 38917

Cover Design by
Bob Horton

PUBLISHER'S INTRODUCTION

In 1977, the Christian Education Committee of Covenant Presbytery published the first thirty questions and answers to this present work. The purpose was to determine if there were sufficient interest to warrant publication of this larger work. The response was significant.

The Committee is now pleased to present Joyce Horton's entire work on the catechism for young children as well as the appendage which deals with establishing and maintaining a catechism program. It is the Committee's hope that this will stimulate catechism instruction in our churches and lead many of our young people to learn the **Westminster Shorter Catechism** as well.

This Committee is deeply indebted to the Women in the Church of Covenant Presbytery for making contributions available for this project.

Christian Education Committee
Covenant Presbytery PCA
Post Office Box 102
Carrollton, Mississippi 38917

AUTHOR'S PREFACE

When the author conducted a series of classes explaining how to teach the **Child's Catechism** to children, the ladies of the First Presbyterian Church, Crystal Springs, Mississippi, recorded and transcribed the talks. Some editing has been done, but the format remains conversational and not consciously literary in style.

No greater privilege or responsibility is given to parents and teachers than that of "training up (the) children" in the "nurture and admonition of the Lord," and few, if any, tools exceed the **Catechism for Young Children** in value for this purpose.

The main thrust of this effort has been to show how the great Biblical doctrines may be put into language comprehensible to children for the effectual communication of God's truths.

My thanks go to Rev. Sam Patterson, Dr. Morton Smith, Dr. Norman Harper, Mrs. Bewey Bowden, Mrs. Wayne Herring, Mrs. Richard Aeschliman, Rev. Bob Hayes, my husband Frank and son Bob, the ladies of the Crystal Springs Presbyterian Church, and the Women in the Church of Covenant Presbytery, for all the help, encouragement, and work that went into this publication.

May the Holy Spirit be pleased to use this material in some way to teach "these little ones" the love of our Lord.

Mrs. Frank C. Horton
704 East Leake Street
Clinton, Mississippi   39056

FOREWORD

There has been such a time lapse between the first teaching of this material and this publication that I want to suggest more material for the teacher to read and to have in his library for reference when teaching the catechism.

I highly recommend **A HARMONY OF THE WESTMINS-TER PRESBYTERIAN STANDARDS** with explanatory notes by J.B. Green for use in teaching baptism, the Lord's supper, the resurrection of the dead and the last judgment, the ten commandments, and the sacraments. However, it is currently out of print. Most ministers and many church libraries will have a copy.

THE LORD'S PRAYER by Dr. Robert J. Ostenson, produced by LOGOI, Inc., Miami, Florida, is a good book to have in your library and to study when teaching the Lord's prayer.

THE TEN COMMANDMENTS by Thomas Watson and **THE TEN COMMANDMENTS** by Arthur W. Pink are both excellent study material for use in teaching the commandments.

Every catechism teacher should have a copy of the Westminster Standards adopted by the Presbyterian Church in America. It includes the Westminster Confession of Faith and the Larger and Shorter Catechisms. It is available through the Christian Education Committee of the P.C.A., 4319 Memorial Drive, Suite F., Decatur, Georgia 30032.

Basic for a Christian teacher's library is a good concordance. **CRUDEN'S COMPLETE CONCORDANCE** is excellent if you can't afford Young's or Strong's. Also you should have at least one good one-volume commentary. I suggest you start with Matthew Henry. As you study and grow, you will want to add other sets of commentaries. Many excellent ones are available. Money spent on good sound commentaries is money well invested.

Mt. Olive Tape Library, P.O. Box 422, Mt. Olive, Mississippi 39119, has excellent tapes at very reasonable rental (or purchase) prices that will help you as the teacher learn the deeper doctrines of the church before trying to teach them. Tapes are available on Christ's Kingly Role by Dr. Morton Smith and Dr. Nigel Lee; Covenantal Theology by Dr. G. VanGroningen and Dr. Palmer Robertson; the Ten Commandments by Dr. R. J. Rushdoony, Dr. Nigel Lee, Pastor Walter Chantry, James Moore, and Sam Patterson; and Biblical Doctrine of Hell by Dr. Al Martin. Other excellent tapes are also available.

Reformed Theological Seminary of Jackson has been of invaluable help to me in my teaching. Call or write the Campus Christian Book Store, 5422 Clinton Blvd., Jackson, Mississippi 39209 (Tel. 601-922-4988) and ask for helpful books on any subject you are teaching or any doctrinal point that is giving you difficulty. This is a wonderful way for a Christian to build up a good home library.

Any good Reformed Christian book store or pastor should be able to help you with book selections helpful to your teaching ministry.

The catechism teacher should take every opportunity to further his own theological education from sound, Reformed sources. The more theology you learn, the more information you have to give to the children, regardless of age. Then all you have to do is learn to cross the language barrier between child and adult, and you'll have a wonderfully blessed ministry.

God bless you!
Joyce Horton

TABLE OF CONTENTS

CATECHISM CLASSES

Q. 1. Who made you?
A. God.

How did He make you? (Pause, for nobody ever answers. For here they're testing the teacher.) Well, how did He make Adam? (Wait for the children to answer.) Yes, He just picked up a handful of dirt and made Adam. How did He make Eve? (Wait for the children to answer.) Yes, He made Eve from the rib of Adam. How did He make you? (Slight pause, don't wait for the answer.) We just aren't really sure that we understand **HOW** He made us. David said in a Psalm that we are "fearfully and wonderfully made!" And that's true, isn't it? What's the first thing little children notice about a baby? The tiny fingers and toes! A little baby fascinates us, for a little baby is just like a miracle. In fact, that is exactly how God made you and me. It is a miracle. We are still made out of dirt, but we are made now with mothers and daddies. A mother and daddy marry and then they have babies, but they can't make babies. Some mothers want babies very much, but they don't get them. Some young people marry and don't want babies because they want to spend their time doing other things besides raising children. Yet they have babies. Why? Who made those babies? God made them! God is the only person who can make a person. (Understand that when I am asking these questions the children are answering them. As they answer they tend to get off the subject. One of the best ways to bring them back is to come back to the original question.) Now, Who made you? God. (You are now ready to go on to the second question. This is the way in which I present the catechism's first question to children in grades one through three.)

If you are teaching fourth through sixth grades, you can start in much the same way to get their interest or their attention. A really important point in teaching children (and this way you gain their interest, love, and respect, or whatever it is a teacher must gain from children to be a successful teacher) is to anticipate their doubts. In teaching this group, start much the same way, and tell them that scientists of today can tell you the correct percentage of every mineral and chemical in our bodies, and yet they can't make a man. They can't give it life. God breathed the breath of life into man, and man became a living soul. So God is the only one who can give life. Now ask: When did God decide to make you? Before the formation of the world. Just imagine! Before He even formed the world, and before He made the Grand Canyon and the Mediterranean Sea, and Mount Everest — and China — He had already decided that He was going to make you. He had decided that He was going to let the world exist for over a thousand years, and He was going to stop having chariots and start having cars, and He was going to start having airplanes, and then He was going to make you! All that time He knew that you were going to be born on a certain day of a certain year in a certain town. How did He know that? Because He planned it. (You cannot start too early to get into the heads of children that God made each of them for a purpose.) If He made you, it is going to follow inevitably that there was a reason. The "Why" is going to come next. He made you for a purpose. It will change your whole life, it will change the way you act, it will change the way you think, if and when you learn that God made you. Now, Who made you? God!

If you are teaching seventh and eighth grades, you are going to anticipate their doubts in order to hold their interest and gain their confidence. What is the first doubt the seventh and eighth graders are going to come up with? They're getting it in school, and it's against the law to teach it! Evolution! All right, How did God make you? Well, I'll tell you a story: Someone in school is going to tell you that He started with this little single cell, and He did all of this monkey foolishness that took Him years and years and years, so that it took God hundreds of years to make you. And finally you became a man. Now we are a really fine, good-looking race of people, aren't we? (Sarcastically, of course!) Of course we started with these (ugh!) hairy, humpbacked, awful-looking old cave men, and that is the best God could do, do you understand? He made a man, but *we* developed and matured until now, and we are a pretty good-looking bunch of folks, you'll have to admit. That is why we have mirrors all over our houses. We just think we're nice-looking folks. All right, but the way the **BIBLE** says He made you is in God's image! And then He looked at man and said that this is very good. Yet the Bible says no man is good! So this Adam that God made was the best-looking specimen of humanity that anybody can imagine. You will never in your life see any man measure up to what Adam was because he was perfect. God made him, and said that His work was very good, and there is no degree of perfection with God. Either it's perfect, or it's no good. So God made a fine man, and he was without fear. Then He made a woman out of Adam's rib, and they were the perfect couple. Adam did not have to lift bar bells like my boy does to build up his body. He was much better-looking than anybody you've ever seen — much stronger and healthier, too. Adam was a wonderful specimen of a man.

Now you are going to have questions about the cave man. But you see, man fell; and God had warned him: "If you sin, you are going to die." God knew that sin would so corrupt the blood of man that he would have a body that would be capable of dying.

You know that we begin to die when we are born: we begin to grow old and die. That's because there's sin in our bodies (or natures) and the Bible says that death is the result of sin. So man degenerated from this perfect man until you find in chapters five and eleven of Genesis that a man lived nine hundred years (he had such a perfect body.) The next generation lived eight hundred years, the next seven hundred, six hundred, and right on down until now the life span is three score years and ten. Man degenerated because of sin until he was a cave man. Men did live in caves — they found the caves with pictures on the walls and man was just no good. He had not given himself to God, and he had not subdued the earth as commanded; he had just lived in his sin until God repented that He had ever made him. God said that He would wipe man off the face of the earth. In the Genesis Flood, the waters of the deep came up, and the waters from above came down, and the tremendous upheaval inside the earth caused the earth to be completely destroyed and made over. There was a new world. So, apparently the cave man lived during the time before the flood. So just set these seventh and eighth graders straight right in the very first place. Who made you? **GOD MADE MAN!** He made him in the image of God; male and female created He them. You as an adult should be able to show to the children a good, healthy, proper respect for this Bible. Don't be one of those that says in answer to their questions, "Well, the Bible said it, honey, and you mustn't question it. You mustn't doubt God's word, etc." **OF COURSE** the Bible says it, and that makes it *true*, but this is a *dynamic* Bible. We Christians aren't stuck with believing some stupid ridiculous idea which is contrary to modern intellect and learning. We believe it because when the Bible is interpreted to us by the Holy Spirit, it is more powerful and marvelous and dynamic than any other book ever written. When God says that He made man, then that is exactly the way it was. God made us!

This is largely the content of what I would say to high schoolers, when teaching the Child's Catechism to them. (And let me say here that this catechism contains so much sound doctrine in basic fundamental principles, that I think it should be taught to and memorized by every child in Presbyterian churches, regardless of age.)

I would approach high schoolers differently, thus: Who made you? God. You believe that? Don't you know the facts of life by now? You are answering this question this way because that is the correct answer according to the book. Not because you believe it. You believe by now that man can govern the number of children he will have, and so you too plan someday to marry and have so many boys and so many girls — no more, no less. So you don't believe that God makes people any more. Oh of course He made Adam! But He didn't make you? Not really! Well, let me tell you something. I've got news for you. God **DID** make you. No human couple on the face of the earth could have planned you and brought you into this world if *God* hadn't meant for you to be here.

(Now proceed with all the interesting things you've taught the others, from the first graders up, to clinch with these sophisticated, worldly high schoolers that you, the teacher, are one jump ahead of them and know what you're talking about!)

Scripture References: Psalm 100:3; Genesis 1:27.

Q. 2. What else did God make?
A. *God made all things.*

The first through third grades will take the teacher's word for it. You know why? Because the teacher looks out the window and says, "He made the trees, and the flowers, and the birds, and the grass," and so the child believes He made everything. But then that first through third grader gets to thinking, and then one day when Mother is just as busy as she can be, he says to her, "Mama, did God make this house?" or "Mother, did God make the cookies?" or "Mother, did God make this shirt?" Mother is so busy she may brush him off with "Yes, honey, God made everything," or she may say, "No, honey, Mother made the cookies," or "No, we bought this house!" or "No, God made the cotton, but a manufacturer made the shirt material and then Mother cut and sewed and made the shirt." Thus too often in the child's mind the catechism teacher has been proven wrong, quite unintentionally. If you're going to teach God's Word you're going to have to teach it straight! So *you* must anticipate the child's doubts. So you ask him, "Well, what about this table? Did God make it? No, but God planted the tree, and made it grow, so that man could cut the tree, saw it, plane it, nail it, and make the table. "Did God make these metal chairs?" No, but God put metal in the ground for man to find and develop. Man never in the world could have made metal the way we find it in the earth; but God put it there. When He made the earth, God put everything into it that man was ever going to need. Then when He made man, He gave him a mind and said to him, "Now you subdue the earth and have dominion over it." That means man has the mind and the challenge from God to develop what God gave him. So Mother made the cookies; and we bought the shirt from the store but the store didn't buy them from God; the store bought them from a manufacturer who cut the material and sewed it and made the shirt. But all of the stuff that is used to make cookies, or clothes, or houses — all of it was put in the earth by God, for us to use. We couldn't make anything if it were not made from what God gave us. So really, God did make everything. What else did God make? God made all things.

In teaching fourth through sixth graders: When they say, "God made all things," you might say, "Well, like what? Just look around this room. Name one thing God made! I don't see a thing God made!" Just push them into telling you the scientific truths that you have told to the little fellows. Otherwise they'll start out with the birds and the grass and the animals, which is all right; but you stop there, and you'll never let those youngsters know that you know as much as they do. One reason some children dislike Sunday School is because the teacher seems so naive!

Now for seventh and eighth graders: I would start by pointing them to Romans, the first chapters, that tell us what a sinner man is, and also tell us that every man can know that there is a God. God has given him two ways to know: by the rule of right or wrong in his heart — God put the law in his heart — and by creation. So it is true, we can look out at creation and see a tree and know that there is, there must be, a God. There is a power that made all of these things. You **MUST** meet seventh and eighth graders on their level, and don't talk down to them. I tell them about one of the best things I ever ran across. It is "The Evolution Protest Movement," Santhia Stoke, Hayling Island, Hants, England. This is a movement by brilliant theologians who have dedicated their lives to disproving evolution, and it is just wonderful! Our children are being taught that every intelligent person believes in evolution. This isn't true! There are many intelligent, brilliant people with degrees of higher education who do not believe the evolution theory. Our children need to know that they too can stand up for the Genesis story of creation without looking or feeling like simpletons, and without being intimidated by **ANYBODY**.

Here is an example of the literature from the Evolution Protest Movement: "Nature teems with such problems. There is the yucca;

a plant which grows wild in Mexico and the southern United States. The flower is so constructed that it can be fertilized by only a peculiar species of moth. The larvae of this moth can live on no other food but the seed of the yucca. Moth and plant are dependent upon each other. The yucca moth has especially contrived tentacles covered with stiff hairs, peculiarly adapted to collect yucca pollen. Mother moth works this up into a ball three times as large as her head. This ball she carefully places on the stigma of another seedcase and she plants two or three eggs among the unripe seeds. She has thus ensured their fertilization and at the same time provided in advance the food essential for her offspring when the eggs hatch. The grubs will not survive and propagate their species without the yucca plant." Is this planned or an accident? Could this beautiful piece of co-operation between insect and plant have evolved by chance variations of mutations?

There are many more interesting examples, about the caterpillar and the ant, and the kangaroo and the whale, and such intricacies and such marvels in nature, that it just makes God bigger. God created it that way.

Scripture References: Acts 17:25; John 1:3; Psalm 33:6-7.

Q. 3. Why did God make you and all things?
A. *For His own glory.*

What is glory? If you don't know, then you don't know why He made you, do you? I guess that "glory" for the first through third grades, is best described by the bright yellow halo that pictures show around Jesus' head. It is His radiance and His brightness. When a child minds, or does something nice, he is letting people see Christ in him. Christ tells us in Matthew, "Let your light so shine that men may see your good works and glorify your Father which is in Heaven." So the good that we do as Christians, as children of God, is to make people know that it is because God loves us and we love God that we do these things. So giving God the glory for something is really giving Him the "credit." Why did God make the trees and the birds and "all things"? Because when we see these things, we know that only God could make them, and so we think about God and His bigness and His greatness and His power. Why did He make you and me? Because He wants people to be able to think about how big and wonderful and powerful He is when they see us. Now if they see us acting mean or ugly or stingily or selfishly or stubbornly, then they don't think about how wonderful God is, do they? They think about the devil! If we act sweet and kind and tender hearted and forgiving and loving, then people think about God and how kind and merciful and loving He is. So we have glorified God by pointing to His goodness. This is what it means to glorify God.

For the older children you are almost forced to start in the same way you did with the little fellows, for this doctrine of being created to God's glory is one of the most tremendous of our Presbyterian theology, and one of the most slighted. Children need to be made conscious of the fact that they didn't just happen into this world, and that they are not the ones to plan what they might happen to want to be when they grow up! Each individual child was put here by God for a specific purpose. That specific purpose will unfold to the child day by day as he learns to lean upon the Lord for guidance and direction. The *general* purpose for everything that he or she does in this life is to glorify God.

There are many parents who glorify their children. You've all seen a busy busy mother; who participates in a wide variety of activities such as Little League Ball, Band Boosters, Girl Scouts, clubs, Glee Club activities, etc., because her child or children are participating in these activities, and she wants to "serve" in this for her children's sake! So she has spent a lot of time glorifying her children, and not actually having as her goal in these activities, glorifying God. In anything we do, the reason behind our doing it determines whether or not we are glorifying God! *Why* does Mother want new furniture? Is it because Daddy is making more money and nicer furniture will testify to their higher social position? Or is it because she knows that new furniture can make the guests of their home more comfortable, and in their way they can serve God as they serve their fellow man? *Why* does Johnny play Little League Baseball? Is it because he truly wants to develop his body, his skill, his personality, his group participation, his friendships with others, for the glory of God? If not, then in all probability he is playing to glorify either himself, the team, or the sport! God **MADE** us so that we might point honor to Him. So everything that we do is to make people conscious of God's presence! Why did God make you? For His glory.

Scripture References: Acts 17:26-27; Revelation 4:11; Psalm 19:1; Isaiah 43:7.

Q. 4. How do you glorify God?
A. *By loving Him and doing what He commands.*

If He made me and determined to put me here at a certain time, then He had a reason, and that was to glorify Himself; now how am I going to glorify Him?

(Well, they have their catechisms in class, open before them, and they'll answer, "By loving Him and doing what He commands.")

First through third graders: *Do* you love God? (Oh yes, they just think He's wonderful.) Do you do what He tells you to do? He tells us in the Bible how He wants us to act, and how to treat other people. In John's letters, He tells us two ways we may know whether or not we are God's children and love Him: One is that we want to do what He commands (or wants us to do), and the other is that we love other people. God tells us in His Bible that if we'll obey what the Bible tells us to do, and be kind to other people, we will be showing God that we love Him.

The children have a song (remind them of it) that begins, "This Little Light of Mine, I'm going to let it shine." This is the light of Christ, shining in you, that points to God, and makes other people know you love Him.

For junior high students you can now give them the plan of salvation, because the answer to this question really involves sanctification. We cannot love God in our own strength or merely by willing to do it. The Bible says that the natural man is at enmity with God. This means that if we are not Christians, we just naturally prefer sin to Christianity. After we are Christians, the "old man" in us is at war with the "new man" to get us to yield in sin. Therefore, I *cannot* love God and do what He commands, but Christ living in me can. When I accept Christ into my heart as my personal Saviour, then the Holy Spirit, the third person of the Trinity, comes into my life and begins the work of enabling me to live the Christian life. Nobody really likes God unless he has the Spirit of God in his heart, for we were not born liking God. Christ in us is the only being that can obey God's commandments in the right way. Christ in you is the only thing in you that can love God and guide you to do good things.

Scripture References: John 6:29; Matthew 5:16.

Q. 5. Why ought you to glorify God?
A. Because He made me and takes care of me.

Of what did He make you? When did He decide to make you? (Here is our second example of how beautifully our catechism builds doctrine upon doctrine already established. Question 3 is built upon the truth of Questions 1 and 2. Question 5 is also built upon the truth of Question 1. For this reason we will go back and review past questions, by rephrasing them and asking questions about them that we have already taught.)

I am to glorify God, that is, do things that will make people see how big and wonderful and marvelous God is, because He is the creator, the one that made me. If He made me, then He made me for His glory, and therefore I ought to do that for which I was made.

The children of all ages know the providential care of God, so they only need to be reminded that another reason we ought to do those things that God has commanded us to do is that He is so good to us in His protection of us. The Bible says we love Him because He first loved us. This, then, is what it means.

Scripture References: Psalm 23; Psalm 139:13-16.

Q. 6. Are there more gods than one?
A. There is only one God.

To be *God* means to have all power. If, then, there were two Gods, one of them would have power over the other. For if they disagree on how to do something, one of them would win over the other, and that would make Him the top God. So of necessity there has to be only one supreme all-powerful God. This need not be explained to the first-through-third graders. It will be good to mention to seventh and eighth graders, as it may plant sound theology in their minds that may enable them to lead some heathen to the Lord some day.

Scripture References: Deuteronomy 6:4; Ephesians 4:5-6.

Q. 7. In how many persons does this one God exist?
A. In three persons.

The hardest thing to teach children is the doctrine of the Trinity. I am a mother, a sister, a daughter, a wife, and an aunt, but still I am only one person. No secular example is sufficient to explain the Trinity. Just tell the little children that God is only one God, but He is still three persons, but the three make up just one God. We can't understand it, but that the Bible tells us that now we don't understand lots of things, but we will understand them when we get to Heaven.

Scripture Reference: I John 5:7.

Q. 8. What are they?
A. The Father, the Son, and the Holy Ghost.

I prefer to teach Questions 7 and 8 together, without stopping to dwell too much on Question 7 by itself. God is three persons. Which one came first? They were all three the same God from the beginning. Is Jesus as old as God the Father? Yes, they are all three the same God. Which one of them made you? The Bible says all three said, "Let *us* make man." Which one of the persons of the Godhead came to earth to die for you? God the Son. God the Son came to die for me; God the Father is the one who answers my prayers through the name of the Son; and God the Holy Spirit comes and lives in me. It is all God.

In the first verse of Genesis, the word "God" is translated from the Hebrew plural word, meaning a plural God. This would be interesting to the seventh and eighth graders. Yet the verb "created" is singular, so that we understand it to mean that the plural persons of the Godhead were all present in the creation. Then Genesis 1:2 says, "And the Spirit of God moved upon the face of the waters," and so here is the Holy Spirit present and at work. God was, from the beginning, Father, Son, and Holy Ghost.

Scripture References: Matthew 28:19; I John 5:7.

Q. 9. What is God?
A. *God is a spirit, and has not a body like men.*

You said that you were made in His image. What does that mean? You have hands and feet, and the Bible says that no man can pluck God's children from His hands. That sounds like God has a hand. Do we look like God? The Bible says in John 4:24, "God is a Spirit, and they that worship Him must worship Him in spirit and in truth." God is not bound by a physical body. He took on a physical body so that He could accomplish the job of redeeming us, but He is not bound by physical limitations and a body. When He made us in His image He gave us souls that could never die. In the Pauline letters, there is a verse that says when you become one of God's children, you must think no more of people as personalities or individuals, but as souls. I cannot say that I can't like a person because of the way she wears her hair, or because I disapprove of the way he spends his time, or that with another there is just a clash of personality. If you look at people as souls, then there are only two kinds of people. What are they? The saved and the lost. If you see someone and see only a lost soul, you try to point them to Christ. If he or she is a saved soul, then you enjoy Christian fellowship with them, regardless of the kind of clothes they wear, or the correctness of their spirituality. If you are the stronger, you can help them. You look at everyone as souls. This is the way God made us in His image. But _He_ is a spirit.

Scripture Reference: John 4:24.

Q. 10. Where is God?
A. _God is everywhere._

This is not difficult for them to understand. I believe all of the children understand this, and if they want to ask you questions about it you can answer them without any trouble, I believe.

Scripture Reference: Psalm 139:7-12.

Q. 11. Can you see God?
A. _No; I cannot see God, but He always sees me._

The correct answer to this question requires a different emphasis. "No, I cannot see God, but He **ALWAYS** sees me. Always! Just imagine! The Bible says that God never sleeps. He's always taking care of me. No wonder He is doing such a good job! No wonder He tells me not to worry! Why should I worry? I have a great big God in Heaven and He is so big He isn't even bound by a human body. He is everywhere! He says that He can see me always! Whoever wrote this must have been a child once himself, for look at the very next question.

Scripture References: Hebrews 4:13; John 2:25; Proverbs 15:3.

Q. 12. Does God know all things?
A. _Yes; nothing can be hid from God._

Why didn't you tell Mother what you did yesterday? Why did you try to hide the bad paper from Daddy? Why did you and your little friends hide to do such and such? You are hiding from human eyes, but you can't hide from God. Then why do you try? And adults are still trying! Why do you try? Because you forget about God and you forget that He is really here all of the time and can see everything. He saw what you were thinking that night you couldn't go right to sleep. Everybody else thought you were asleep but God. We can't even hide what we are thinking from Him. Why do we forget that? It is because we don't love Him enough and we don't think about Him enough. If we would think about God more, then we would be more conscious of what we are doing and of the fact that God is seeing it and knowing it. We would try harder to please Him.

We need to have a bigger God ourselves before we present Him to our children. I think that I know the catechism pretty well, but I don't ever try to teach children without studying my Bible some more and praying some more. I have to learn something new about God and it has to be fresh to me before I can give it to them. You will be amazed to learn how hungry they are for the Word. Stand up and tell them what a big God they have, and what sinners we are!

Scripture References: Psalm 139; Acts 15:18; Hebrews 4:13.

Q. 13. Can God do all things?
A. Yes; God can do all His holy will.

Can God tell a lie? No! I thought you said He could do anything? God can't do anything bad! God can only do perfect things, good things. Now that is going to disappoint the children. Because they are not so holy that they like the things of God. You don't like the things of God any better than I do: if you did you'd be doing them. He says things in the Bible for me to do that just don't appeal to me at all! This child has to keep a big God, and you can't tear down his idea of God with this question. He has to see that anything God cannot do does not make Him smaller.

For instance, you have a child that just loves his daddy, and he thinks his daddy can do anything. He doesn't have to worry about homework, because his daddy will help him. His daddy can teach him to swim, his daddy can do anything that seems great to the child. If you hear of a man that stole $1,000 from a bank, would your daddy be a bigger man if he stole $2,000, or if he didn't steal any? You hear of a man who murders somebody. Would your daddy be a better man if he murdered two people, or if he didn't murder any? No, you don't have to be able to do bad things to be bigger than the man who does bad things. The goodness of God makes Him bigger than the badness of man. Let your child see that it is the goodness of God that makes Him perfect.

No, He can't lie, and we are thankful that He can't, because if He could, how would I know that He would take care of me? He says He will in His Bible, but how would I know whether I could believe Him? But everything He has promised me in this Bible is true. It is bigger and better than anything the world can promise you.

To do good for His children, then, is the holy will of God. He can do anything good that He wills to do! He can do anything He wants to do, but He can't do anything wrong.

What is "holy"? "Holy" means dedicated to God. Any will is holy that is dedicated to making God more wonderful to you. "Holy Bible" means the book dedicated to God. How many of you are keeping the Sabbath day — the whole Sunday — not just Sunday morning — dedicated to God?

In teaching the meaning of the word "holy" to the seventh and eighth graders, refer them to Romans 12:1, "Present your bodies a living sacrifice, holy, acceptable unto God." Then let these children know that even their bodies must be dedicated to God. Your body is the temple of God and you must keep it holy all of the time. That is what God requires.

Scripture References: Ephesians 1:11; Hebrews 6:18; Philippians 2:13.

Q. 14. Where do you learn how to love and obey God?
A. *In the Bible alone.*

Why don't you say "in Sunday School" or "in Catechism Class" or "from Mother and Daddy"? Because the Bible is the only place that we have the pure Word of God. When a person gives you their interpretation of it or their understanding of it, it is not pure any longer, because it is second hand — it has come through an unclean vessel. Some put in their own ideas, because no person fully understands the whole Bible. But when you go to the pure Word, you can be taught by the Holy Ghost. God gave the Word and He preserved it, and it is pure and perfect. We have an example in Acts where the people went home and studied the Word to see if what the preacher was preaching was truth. That is what every person ought to do. When you learn these things, go to your Bible to check them out. One way to go to your Bible is to ask the teacher what Scripture she has to back up the statements she made. What Scripture teaches that God is a spirit? What Scripture teaches that God is in three persons? What we're teaching must be based on the Bible. God's Word alone is the only sure way to learn how to love and obey God.

Scripture References: Galatians 1:8-9; II Timothy 3:16; John 17:17.

Q. 15. Who wrote the Bible?
A. *Holy men who were taught by the Holy Ghost.*

What kind of men wrote the Bible? Holy men. That doesn't mean men that can sit on nails and not get hurt. It doesn't mean supernatural men. A holy person is a person dedicated to God. God says for us to be holy. But the men who wrote the Bible were men not only dedicated to God, but men who were taught by the Holy Ghost, the third person of the Trinity. So holy men of old spake as they were moved by the Holy Ghost, and wrote our Holy Scriptures.

Scripture References: II Peter 1:21; II Timothy 3:16.

Review

Who made you? God did.

When did God plan to make you? Before the foundation of the world. He decided each individual life and what He wanted done with that life, even before He formed the world. Who makes all babies? Who is responsible? Who is the only one that can really create life? God. If we get it into our heads that God made us, then it will make a big difference in our lives. This will make a big difference in the lives of young people right now, when they reach the marrying age. It will make a difference to parents to know that this is in God's hands. Who decides how many children each family is going to have? God. For what did He make you? Always anticipate their doubts, and word the question in a different way to keep them thinking. You don't want the catechism to be so parroted that when you ask a question they know the answer by words alone, and it does not have any meaning to them. Of course if they learn the words now, later they will get the meaning, but if you can give them the meaning now they are years ahead in their knowledge of God.

So, for Question 3 you can say, "Well, why did God do that?" That wakes them up. What else did God make— God made all things. Why did He make you and all things? For His own glory. How can you glorify God? By loving Him and doing what He commands. We learn that these are the two things in which Christ summed up all of the commandments. One is to love the Lord and one is to be obedient. These two include all of the other commandments.

Why ought you to love and glorify God? Because He made you and takes care of you. How does God take care of you? God has guardian angels to take care of us, and in Deuteronomy He says that underneath are the "everlasting arms." In John 10:28 He says, "And I give unto them eternal life; and they shall never perish, neither shall any man pluck them out of my hand." (These side questions are related, but they are to keep the child's interest.) When He says that He will take care of you, that means that He won't let anything bad happen to you at all. Is that what it means?

That is not what it means. What does it mean? It means that He is there holding you and taking care of you His way and lets only those things happen to you that He plans. No matter how bad these things are, He promises that He will never leave you and He has you in the shadow of His wing. He is taking care of you through trouble. He is making your spirit grow. He does not say that He is going to take the trouble completely away. Then, why ought you to glorify God? Because He made you and takes care of you.

How many Gods are there? There is only one God. This is one of the greatest statements of Scripture. "Hear, O Israel: The Lord our God is one Lord." This is a statement with which children will not have any trouble.

How many persons are in this one God? Three. I John 5:7.

What are these persons? Father, Son, and Holy Ghost.

Which one came first? All of them were from the beginning.

Which one made you? All.

What are they doing now? It helps children to get this picture, although it may be oversimplification. The Father is on the throne in Heaven and Christ is sitting on the right hand of God. What is He doing? He is interceding for us, praying for the saints. It is a good thing for children to feel that every time the devil comes to God and says, "I saw John do so and so and his family does not know it, but I saw it," that Christ is sitting right there and saying, "But I died for John, and he can come to Heaven and live with us even if he did that — if he believes that I died for him."

Where is the Holy Spirit? He is in our hearts. How does He get there? By our receiving Him. We need to open the doors of our hearts through prayer and ask Him in.

What is God? God is a spirit, and has not a body like men. Does that mean He is a ghost? To a child that makes him the invisible body of a dead person. A ghost implies something that has been dead and carries an eerie feeling. Yes, a spirit is a ghost — but God is the only one. There are no spirits or ghosts of dead persons such as you see in shows or comic books. We want to get across the true meaning that He is not bound by a body. The reason the Bible says we are under the shadow of His wing, or mentions the "eye" of God and other parts of the body, is that the little mind of man is trying to comprehend the love, the protection, and the mercy of God. These words are used for our help, but not to have us limit God to a body. He is a spirit and can be everywhere.

Can you see God? No, I cannot see God, but He always sees me. Did He see any of you at school last week? Did He see you after you went home? You all sinned between the last class and this class, didn't you? When you sin, what do you do about it? Do you confess it, say you are sorry and ask for forgiveness, and ask strength not to do it again? This is confession for cleansing, repentance, and sanctification. Ask that the Holy Spirit will live in you and keep you from doing it again.

Does God know all things? Yes, nothing can be hid from God — not even the things that we think, nor the things that we would like to do but do not have the nerve to do. He knows all of those things. Can God do all things? Yes, God can do all His holy will. "Holy" is "dedicated to God." Can God do bad things? Can He lie? Does that make Him bigger or smaller? It makes Him a bigger God because He can't compromise with sin. We can compromise with sin, but the fact that He can do only those things that are good makes Him a big God to us.

And where do you learn how to love and obey God? In the Bible alone. Teachers, what does "obey" mean? It means "mind." It means to love and mind God. We learn how to obey God in the Bible alone because that is the inspired Word of God. We learn it through our preachers and teachers only insofar as they are teaching it the way the Bible says it. That is the reason for having your Scripture references and giving them to the children along with the catechism answers. I think it is good to remind the children of what the minister says on Sunday morning. After reading the Scripture he says, "And may the Holy Spirit interpret to us the meaning of this Word." He can't preach the Bible effectively unless the Holy Spirit, who wrote it, interprets it to us. Open every class with prayer, that the Holy Spirit will teach these children. This does not mean that they don't have to listen to you! Ephesians 4 teaches us that God raised some to be teachers. God can and does teach through the teacher, but the final answer and the final authority for everything we teach lies in the Bible, not in the

catechism. The catechism is merely a way to learn the Bible.
Who wrote the Bible? Holy men taught by the Holy Ghost.
Remind them again what "holy" means — dedicated to God! Get
the meaning of this word so well drilled into their thinking that they
will stop and think of the meaning every time they run into the
word, for many Scriptures will take on deeper meaning for them as
they come to realize what this word means.

Q. 16. Who were our first parents?
A. *Adam and Eve.*

For the first through third graders you explain that "parent"
means mothers and daddies, and that everybody on earth came
from Adam and Eve. They were the first humans on this earth; they
had children, and their children had children, and their children
had children and so on, right down to us today. This is a fascinating
thought to children to realize that everybody is kin to each other!
Yes, the Bible says that God made of one blood all nations. All the
red and yellow, black and white were created by the same God
and have one set of parents — Adam and Eve. If they ask how they
got to be different colors, you have the story of the Tower of Babel
to explain that the same God who could start them all out alike
could confuse their languages and give them different racial traits
as He scattered them abroad upon the face of the earth. I have
heard it interestingly explained that the African was given black,
curly, thick hair to protect him from the hot tropical sun, and the
oriental's diet which is so different from ours may have been
responsible for the development of certain of his characteristics.
This type of information, however, is based on studies other than
the Bible. The important **FACT** for us to present to children is that
Adam and Eve were really persons and had many children over
many, many years and that **ALL** the human race came from them.
Your first through third graders will very likely accept this with no
question asked.
Fourth through sixth graders may ask who Cain married. If they
don't ask you, you anticipate the fact that someone sooner or later
is going to plant this question in their minds, so remind them that

Adam and Eve lived about nine hundred years and begat sons and daughters. As Acts 17:26 teaches us that *all* mankind descended from Adam and Eve, we have **NO** alternative but to believe that Cain married one of Adam and Eve's children or grandchildren. Any of the other ideas brought forth are not Scriptural.

That is one of the important reasons for the whole catechumen program: If you, as a sound, conservative teacher of the Bible, can get to them **FIRST** with the truths of the Gospel, they are not likely to be swayed by false doctrine when they do hear it presented in later years. In other words, if they are taught later that Adam and Eve were not really the first humans but merely were representatives of "humanity," or that God created "other" people and that is where Cain got his wife, these teaching will not "throw" them or sway them if they can remember that as children in catechism class they were **WARNED** that someday they would be faced with these heresies. So as you teach catechism, give to the children a good healthy respect for the Bible as God's Word and the absolute, final authority.

I was taught the "Bible stories" as a child, but when I became a freshman in a very liberal, church-related college, I believed everything my college teachers taught me. I felt sure these people knew more than those who had just taught me to believe what the Bible said! I thought my mother was certainly "way behind the times," for she didn't have any idea how much of this book wasn't so, and I spent a great deal of my time at home explaining to her the myths, legends, and errors that I had learned were so rampant in the Bible! Well, she took care of that! She spent a great deal of her time explaining to me, too! But I think it is really important to anticipate what these children are going to meet in the world, and to stay one jump ahead!

When teaching this question to seventh and eighth graders, tell them that when they get to college they are going to have teachers tell them that Adam and Eve were not really individual people, but represent "mankind." Many, many grown people don't believe the literal story of the creation of Adam and Eve. Do you? Do you believe it? Why do you believe it? God says it is so. It is in the Bible, and we have learned that men dedicated to God spake and wrote as they were guided and directed **BY THE HOLY GHOST**, who is **GOD HIMSELF**! How could you prove it to someone who did not believe it? Of course you believe it because the Holy Spirit has opened your understanding to enable you to receive the truths of God, and if they don't believe it, it is because the same God who revealed it to you has blinded their eyes so that they cannot believe it. If they cannot believe it, then you can't prove it to them and make then accept it. But you can present the logic of it! The Bible tells us to be ready at all times to give an account or reason for the hope that is within us. Be ready to defend intelligently and Scripturally your beliefs. But of those others the Bible also says, "By wisdom they know not God." And sometimes, in their own minds, they're just too "smart" to believe the teachings in the Bible.

I think that the lineages in the Bible are interesting at this point. Ususally we read over the "begat" chapters as very uninteresting, but the Lord went into great detail to give us the family tree! Matthew 1 traces Christ back to Abraham. Luke traces Christ back to Adam. Most people have no trouble believing there was a man named Noah; then who was Noah's father? Terah. Who was Terah's father? And his father? The Bible gave their names in every generation, back to Adam. If Adam wasn't a man, where did Seth come from? Who was Seth's father? The Bible says that it was Adam, and that God made Adam, the first man on earth.

Scripture References: Genesis 3:20; Acts 17:26.

Q. 17. Of what were our first parents made?
A. *God made the body of Adam out of the ground, and formed Eve from the body of Adam.*

Now let one of the children tell the story of God's putting Adam to sleep and taking out a rib from which to make Eve.

Why didn't God just make Eve out of dirt also? If you had a lump of clay and you made something out of it, then you pinched off part of it and smoothed that spot over and made something else, you'd know you made both objects from the same clay. It is all one.

That is what God did. Genesis 2:24 says, "Therefore shall a man leave his father and his mother, and shall cleave unto his wife: and they shall be one flesh." The reason God made the woman from the man was to show us for all time that there is no way a court or anything else can separate that man and woman. They are ONE in God's eyes. Christ said it very plainly, and He said that it is a hard thing for a man to accept, but we MUST get across to the children a good, healthy, honorable attitude toward marriage, based on the fact that God created woman from the man. In His eyes they are one.

I Timothy tells us why the woman can't be the leader. Why don't we have women elders? Why aren't the women the leaders of the church or the nation? Or the home? God gives two reasons: (1) The woman was made the helpmate for the man. He's to be the leader; she's to be his helper! (2) She would lead astray. That will come later when we study the temptation. Why didn't Adam eat of the fruit first and then tempt Eve? Eve tempted him to do wrong, and the Bible tells us that the woman will lead in the wrong direction. She's incapable of being the leader according to God's requirements.

With little first through third graders, I would not go into the divorce issue on this question, for if they are from divorced parents, it will only upset them. But your seventh and eighth graders need to know it, and I personally believe it should be taught to the fourth through sixth graders. We are not judging or condemning their parents. If they have sinned, perhaps they have already asked forgiveness. We are sinners, too, so we aren't making them worse sinners than anyone else; but we must teach the children for their own future's sake that God has set forth definite facts regarding marriage. It is tremendously important for them to know that God created Eve from Adam! I have seen only one person in my life who really trained her children on this principle. She had a married son, and coming home after the war from overseas, he called her when he hit American soil and told her he would be home soon. By coming only a hundred miles out of his way he could stop off at her house, spend the night, then go on to his wife and baby. And she said, "No! Don't you come to see me before you have seen your wife and baby first." She gave him this Scripture saying you leave your mother and father and cleave to your wife, for she is first with you now. That does not mean that you don't honor your parents. We never outgrow honoring our parents. The Bible says we are to take care of them. But the husband is to know that his first loyalty is to the wife, for they are one in God's eyes.

Scripture References: Genesis 2:7; Genesis 2:21-23; Genesis 3:19; Psalm 103:14.

Q. 18. What did God give Adam and Eve besides bodies?
A. *He gave them souls that could never die.*

By the way, be sure the children always answer verbatim. They must give the exact wording of the answers. In answering, "What else did God make?" they are likely to say, "All things." Make them say, "God made all things." In answering what God gave Adam and Eve besides bodies, they may say, "Souls that could never die." Make them say, "He gave them souls that could never die." You want them to memorize the correct wording of the whole catechism, but you also want them to understand the sense of it.

I would not stop with Question 18, but go ahead and connect Questions 18, 19, and 20, for I believe this is the best way for them to understand what a soul is.

Scripture Reference: Genesis 2:7.

Q. 19. Have you a soul as well as a body?
A. *Yes; I have a soul that can never die.*

Scripture Reference: Genesis 2:7.

Q. 20. How do you know that you have a soul?
A. *Because the Bible tells me so.*

(The catechism you are using may have "Because I can think about God and the world to come.

The Bible tells us that we are made in the image of God. This is what sets us apart from animals, and makes us different from all other creatures. How does having a soul make you different? Because your pet can't think about God, can it? Your kitty is fun to play with, but when it dies it does not have a soul that goes to Heaven. We adults must stop teaching our children that there is an animal heaven for pets, for this is unscriptural. We must never be guilty of teaching a lie in the pragmatic belief that it eases the child's hurts over the death of a pet! Whenever my father got me a new puppy, he would remind me that I was not to love my pet as a person, because it was not **LIKE** a person, and I was not to mourn over its death as I would over the death of a person. I never met another child during my childhood that was taught that way, but I learned to appreciate that teaching very much.

Remind your older children that it is *because* God made man in His own image that He demands the death penalty in the case of murder! It is *because* God made man in **HIS** image, giving him a soul that could never die, that He requires the death of the person who attacks another person, for he has attacked the very image of God! Remind your class that capital punishment was ordained by God, and no modern lawmaking body has any right to change that law.

This does not mean, however, that your soul is your brain. Smaller children are likely to get this confused. It is true that you have a brain. But your soul is that invisible part of you that God made capable of comprehending that there is a great, powerful, divine God that created the heavens and the earth, and all that in them is! You were made in God's image, and God is a spirit, so your spirit is that invisible part of you that can think about God and the world to come.

The Bible also tells us that God's power and deity are made known to all human beings. Therefore, we are without excuse if we don't worship Him as the true God. The Bible tells us that God showed man, through the works of nature and creation, that there is a powerful, divine God. God made people in such a way that all mankind **KNOW** there is a God greater than we are. He gave us minds or spirits with the capacity to think and reason and meditate. You can train animals to respond to stimuli, but they don't reason or meditate. God made man with the ability to think about God and the life to come. That is why the person who has never heard of the Bible or Jesus still believes in a life hereafter, and makes crude preparation for it. Sometimes he has buried with him things that he thinks he will need in the next world. No animal does this, only man. This is because God *made* man with this potential of knowing there is a God and an afterworld.

How do we **KNOW** absolutely without a doubt that this is so? Because the Bible tells us that we are made in the image of God, and that His power and deity are shown to us and made known to us through nature and creation. We are able to "perceive" or "comprehend" or "understand" that there is a great God creator. He set man over the animal kingdom to subdue it and have dominion over it. Man, redeemed by the blood of Christ, has a future life in Heaven awaiting him at death, and he is able to **KNOW** this because he has a soul, as the Bible tells him.

Scripture References: Genesis 1:26-27; 9:6ff.; Acts 17:22-23; Romans 1:19-20; 13:1-4.

Q. 21. In what condition did God make Adam and Eve?
A. *He made them holy and happy.*

What does "holy" mean? Dedicated to God. Everything that Adam and Eve did and thought was dedicated to God. Do you realize there is no middle ground between sin and glorifying God? There is one line that goes right down the middle, and everything on one side is sin and everything on the other is to God's glory. What you do may be harmless in itself but if you do it for pleasure, that's satisfying the lust of the flesh. It is sin. If you did it to glorify God, it is holy, for it was an act dedicated to God. And it can be exactly the same act! The attitude of the heart toward that act, then, determines whether it is right or wrong unless, of course, it is something specifically required or prohibited in the Scriptures. This is one of the strongest teachings of our church, and I would say teach it to every age and let them absorb as much of it as they can. Everything that you do either glorifies God or it doesn't. Anything at all that you do that is not to glorify God is to satisfy self, or family, or in some way puts another god on the throne. We can rationalize about this from now on, and it still comes out the same. Adam and Eve were created holy, and they were created happy. Happiness, then, is a result of being holy. They were created holy and happy, and they walked with God and they talked with Him and, until the fall, everything they did was in communion with God.

Scripture References: Genesis 1:27, 31; 2:25; Ephesians 4:24.

Here also we begin our cross-references. That is, we refer to a previous question to explain more fully the present one. Here we refer to Question 3. We are created for God's glory, and Adam and Eve glorified God in a state of holiness and happiness. The more man is dedicated to God, the more he will glorify God and his happiness will be a result of his glorifying God. Then will he be able to rejoice in all things, for he will know the supreme truth of Romans 8:28.

Q. 22. What is a covenant?
A. *An agreement between two or more persons.*

This is self explanatory. The two references given are to the covenant with Abraham. I chose these two references because God specifically says, "This will be a sign of our covenant." and sets forth the provisions or requirements that show what a covenant is.

Scripture References: Genesis 9:12; Genesis 17:10.

Q. 23. What covenant did God make with Adam?
A. *The covenant of works.*

This means that God and Adam made an agreement, and in it Adam was supposed to **DO** something. Just give this brief explanation to all ages — don't assume that anybody knows it.

Scripture Reference: Genesis 2:16-17.

Q. 24. What was Adam bound to do by the covenant of works?
A. To obey God perfectly.

What does "bound" mean? It means what did he have to do, or what was he supposed to do, or what was he required to do, or what was demanded and expected of him? Explain the word to the children, especially first through sixth graders. Many of them will know what the word means, but to stop and explain it and put it in other words makes them **THINK** about it. To "obey" means what? To mind. To mind God how? *Perfectly.* That means everything He says do, do exactly the way He says do it. Much of what happened in the Old Testament, especially regarding the laws and sacrifices, was teaching this one thing — that there is a right way to serve God, and there is a wrong way. God wants us not only to obey Him but to obey Him His way. So we must obey God perfectly — that means in every little detail and with the proper attitude! All this is what Adam was supposed to do, or was required to do.

Scripture Reference: Genesis 2:16-17.

Q. 25 What did God promise in the covenant of works?
A. To reward Adam with life if he obeyed Him.

God promised to reward Adam with life if he minded God. What does "reward" mean? To give him something nice, much like a little extra bonus. When you receive a reward, you get something nice for doing what you were supposed to do anyway. If your father gives you money for making good grades, you should have made them anyway. If you return something that was lost to the correct owner and they give you a reward, they give you something you didn't deserve because you should have returned it anyway. They don't have to give you anything but they give you something nice. If Adam minded God perfectly, then God was going to give him life. What kind of life? Well, he wouldn't have had to die. He would have been here all the time. He would never have had to know what physical death was. That is what God promised him.

Scripture References: Genesis 2:16; Genesis 3:22-24.

Q. 26. What did God threaten in the covenant of works?
A. *To punish Adam with death if he disobeyed.*

What does "threaten" mean? It means to say you are going to do something bad. If Mother threatens you with punishment, that means something bad is coming. If she promises you a reward, that means something good is coming. God threatened to punish Adam with death if he disobeyed Him. Did Adam die the day he disobeyed God? No! Then the devil was right, wasn't he? Adam did not get death when he disobeyed God. Oh, yes, he did get death, for his body began to die and sin corrupted the blood stream of humanity. We talked about the life-span of the generations being shortened. It is because sin entered the human body and now the body gets sick and dies. There is not a human body that is exempt from the penalty of death so we die a physical death as a result of this broken covenant, but we do not have to die a spiritual death. The truth of the covenant is that if you don't obey God perfectly you are doomed to Hell. That is eternal or spiritual death.

If you do obey God perfectly you will live forever, so Adam and Eve did not have to die physically or spiritually. They could have lived forever on this earth. This was a beautiful earth. There were not any thorns or weeds, and there was no plowing. All they were expected to do was dress the garden and keep it for God's glory. But God threatened that if Adam did not obey Him perfectly, Adam would die. His body would die; his body would die physically, and spiritually he would go to Hell. But in the covenant,

God Himself planned a way of escape. He made a way for man to escape his own sinful nature. He says that, for the rest of time, death will remain the penalty for sin. But God will pay it Himself! Then we can come to God through the blood of Christ.

For the child this is difficult to understand, and I can't say that he will understand it perfectly; but you present the plan of salvation, and when you do so the Holy Spirit will use it in that life in His own good time. Every opportunity that you have, present the plan of salvation, for we are here for the salvation of souls and the edification of the saved.

So death is the penalty and our bodies die because our bodies are sinful, but we don't have to die the second death. We can live — we can claim the promise of the eternal life — by what? By believing that Jesus Christ died for us and paid the death penalty for us.

Scripture Reference: Genesis 2:17.

Now connect Questions 23 through 26. Explain it in your own words and get the children to explain it in their own words. This is the covenant of works, and when you ask what the covenant of works is, the children should be able to tell you in their own words. This is important in being sure they are understanding it.

The covenant of works was an agreement between God and Adam. God said that if Adam would mind Him perfectly, and never make a single mistake, then God would reward him with eternal life, but if Adam did not mind God perfectly, then God would punish Adam by letting him die.

Q. 27. Did Adam keep the covenant of works?
A. *No; he sinned against God.*

When we asked one little boy this question, he said, "No, he gave it back to God." The answer, of course, is "No, he sinned against God." This means that Adam did not keep his part of the agreement. He did not obey God perfectly. This is sin.

Scripture Reference: Genesis 3:6.

Q. 28. What is sin?
A. *Sin is any want of conformity unto, or transgression of, the law of God.*

Scripture References: James 4:17; I John 3:4.

Q. 29. What is meant by want of conformity?
A. *Not being or doing what God requires.*

What does "want" mean? If you want something, what does that mean? It means you don't have it, doesn't it? "Want" means "lack." If you want candy, it's because you lack as much as you desire. So "want" also means "desire." Want of conformity means you lack conformity or don't have conformity. What is conformity? It means to act like or take on the form of something else. The Bible says we are not to be conformed "to this world, but are to be *transformed* by the renewing of our minds." In this verse "conform" means to act like those around, to act according to your environment.

You probably are going to have to give them an illustration to clarify this question, but I think it is very important that they understand it. For instance: Take a plate: Saran will conform to the shape of the plate. Why? Because it is soft, pliable, easy to handle. It will take on the shape of the plate, or "conform" to the shape of the plate. Now take a small piece of plywood, and put it on that plate. Will it conform to the shape of the plate? No! Why not? It isn't pliable. It won't yield. You sing, "Have Thine own way, Lord, have Thine own way. Thou art the potter, I am the clay. Mold me and make me after Thy will, while I am waiting, yielded and still." The thing that conforms has to be pliable enough to take on the form of the object to which it is conforming.

The Bible says we must not be so pliable that we take on the actions and manner of the world. Then when the world misbehaves at parties you misbehave at parties, because you don't want people mockingly saying, "He's a Sunday School Kid." "He's a sissy." So you conform to the way of the world. Romans says that is not the thing to do. But the Bible also says not to lack or "want" for conformity to the will of God. If this plate represents the will of God, then you have to be so pliable that you fit. That is what we are to do — to seek to conform to the will of God. Romans 9 teaches us yieldedness to the will of God, through the example of the potter and the clay. We are to be yielded to God so that He can mold us into conformity to His will. "Want of conformity" means not fitting the mold of the law of God. It means not being or doing what God requires.

"Requires" means "wants you to do," or "demands of you." When Mother requires you to make up your bed, that is the law. You may not do it every day, but the reason is want of conformity to the law Mother set up. God requires you not to lose your temper — not get mad at anyone — turn the other cheek — let them run over you. You are not going to do it, are you? Why? Because you don't conform to what God requires.

Now give some examples. Daddy says for you to mow the grass when you get home from school and you forget. What is that? Want of conformity. You didn't do what your Daddy required. Mother bakes a cake and tells you to take it to a neighbor and you don't take it. That is want of conformity. You didn't do what Mother required, and of course if you are disobeying your parents, you are sinning, for God's law requires that you obey your parents. Now let the children give you some illustrations. "Mother told me not to go swimming and I went anyway." No, that is transgression, not want of conformity. Think of another example. Let them give you some examples, and you give them some. Hammer and hammer and hammer at their understanding that want of conformity means not being or doing what God requires. It seems to take a long time, even with older children.

Scripture Reference: James 4:17.

Q. 30. What is meant by transgression.
A. *Doing what God forbids.*

I think this may be a poor way of doing it, but it seems to work for me anyway. I tell the children that we are going to have our first lesson in Latin, because you can better understand "transgression" when you understand the Latin words from which it comes. "Trans" means across. What is *trans*portation"? It is a way of going from one place to another, or taking something from one place to another, going across space. What is "*trans*continental"? The *trans*continental airlines go across the continent. To translate a language means to carry it across from one language to another. So "trans" in all of these words comes from the Latin word meaning across. Have the children give some examples using words with "trans" in them. "Gress" means going. "Progress" means going forward; "regress" means going backward. "Digress" means to go away from. See if the children can think of examples. Be sure they understand what "gress" means. You have to understand that it means that act of going across, before you understand what transgression is.

In His Word there are many things the Lord tells us to do. He tells us to be kind to one another; love the brethren; turn the other cheek; lend to him that borroweth not expecting it back. There is a line the Lord has drawn which I call God's "don't" line. "Thou shalt not." You stop short of that line! When you cross it you have transgressed! "Gress" means going. So transgress means to go across God's "don't" line. The Lord said Adam should not eat of the fruit of the tree of knowledge. Adam crossed the line. He and Eve did eat. Their sin was not one of want of conformity, but of transgression.

Now give the children more examples of transgression. Mother has baked another cake and told you not to cut it, and you cut it anyway. You crossed the "do not" line so you have sinned a sin of transgression. Daddy says "don't go out to play until you have practiced your music" and you disobey him. Is this want of conformity or transgression? It is transgression, because it is going across the "don't" line. It is doing what God forbids.

"Forbids" means "tells you not to do", or "demands that you not do," or "doesn't allow." "Forbids" means you are denied the privilege. If mother forbids your staying up late, she has made the law or ruling that demands that you go to bed early. She has said that you shall not stay up late. Therefore when we are doing what God forbids, we are doing those things that God has told us in His Word we are not to do. We are not to steal. If we do, we are transgressing. We are not to tell a lie. If we do, we are transgressing, or going across the "don't" line.

Aside from the two elements in our definition of sin, there is really no other possible sin you can commit. Either you don't do what you are told to do, or you do what you were told not to do. Transgression is to do what God told you not to do; and want of conformity is not to do what God told you to do. Want of conformity is not being yielded to the will of God. Keep on giving the children illustrations of both, and letting them give you illustrations of both, until you see that they are understanding both points. It is very important to get this teaching across. It may not get through to all of your first graders, but third graders and up should be able to understand it; although this one teaching may take longer than any other in the whole catechism.

Scripture Reference: I John 3:4.

Now take Questions 28 through 30 as a unit and have the children give them to you in their own words. Sin is lack of or not being or doing what God wants you to do, or doing what God says not to do. Always give them examples.

Q. 31. What was the sin of our first parents?
A. Eating the forbidden fruit.

Who were our first parents? Adam and Eve. (This will be a cross reference to Question 16.) What does "forbidden" mean? It means that which is not allowed. What kind of fruit was it? No, it wasn't an apple. We don't know what it was, but evidently it was a different kind of fruit from any we know — we are told only that they took of the fruit and ate it. When we say it was an apple, we are just using an example. God had told them not to do it, and they did it anyway. Was this a sin of want of conformity or transgression? It was transgression, because they went across the "thou shalt not" line, and did what God forbade. I Timothy, the second chapter, tells us that Eve was first in the *transgression*.

Scripture References: Genesis 2:17; Genesis 3:1-6.
Cf. Questions: 16, 30.

Q. 32. Who tempted them to this sin?
A *The devil tempted Eve, and she gave the fruit to Adam.*

What does "tempted" mean? The older children may know but the smaller ones may not. It means tried to make them do wrong, or tested. You might say there are two meanings of "tempted." When God told Abraham to take his son up the mountain and kill him, He was not trying to make him do wrong. He was testing him. James says, "Blessed is the man that endureth temptation, for when he is tried, he shall receive the crown of life, which the Lord hath promised to them that love him." Another meaning of "tempted" is trying to make someone do wrong, and that is what the devil does. So the devil tempted Eve and she gave the fruit to Adam and thus tempted him. Eve was first in the transgression.

Who led Christ into the wilderness to be tempted? The Holy Spirit! But who did the tempting? The devil. It would appear, then, the Lord might lead us into a position where the devil would tempt us to wrong, and in this way the Lord is testing us — because the trial of your faith worketh patience, etc. Here again, it is through resisting these temptations that we grow spiritually stronger. We are told never to say that God tempts us, for God tempts no man; but at the same time Christ taught us to ask in the Lord's Prayer that the Lord lead us not into temptation, but deliver us from evil. What we are asking, then, is that the Lord remember our weaknesses and not lead us into testing faster than we are growing, or into situations in which the devil can tempt us beyond our endurance. God has promised strength sufficient to meet these temptations but we still pray that He will be merciful in His leading and in the testing.

For the first through third graders, it will be sufficient to stop with the explanation that "tempted" means tried to make you do wrong.

Scripture References: Genesis 3:1-6; I Timothy 2:14.

Q. 33. What befell our first parents when they had sinned?
A Instead of being holy and happy, they became sinful and miserable.

"Befell" means happened to. What is "holy?" Dedicated to God. Instead of being dedicated to God and happy, they became sinful — they didn't do what God wanted them to do, and they became miserable. What does "miserable" mean? It means to feel just awful — terrible. There is nothing nice or pleasant or happy about being miserable. Miserable is the very opposite of happy. To be miserable is to be completely unhappy.

Scripture References: Genesis 3:16-19, 24.
Cf. Question: 21.

Q. 34. Did Adam act for himself alone in the covenant of works?
A No; he represented all his posterity.

That means when Adam and Eve broke the covenant and sinned against God, were they the only ones to suffer the punishment? Or were they the only ones who would have been rewarded if they had not broken it? No, everybody who came from them suffers. "Represented" means acted for or acted in place of. When the Clinton High ball team wins a game folks say, "Clinton won!" Now I live in Clinton and you live in Clinton and we didn't win because we didn't play! But we are "represented" by the ball team of Clinton High School, and so we say, "We won!" Did Adam act for himself alone in the covenant of works? No, he acted for, or represented somebody. Who? All his posterity.

"Posterity" means everybody who came from them. He represented all of us, because his sinful blood is in all of us and we are born sinners. We are born now with the desire to sin and the Bible tells us that the natural man is at enmity with God. There is nothing about the natural man that would make him want to be a Christian. We love sin. We inherited Adam's sinful nature. We are Adam's posterity. Your children, and your grand-children, and their children and their great-grand-children and on and on for all the generations which come from you are your "posterity." Everybody that comes as your descendant will be your "posterity." Everyone that came after Adam is his "posterity," and that includes everybody. Christ is the only one who was perfect, but He didn't have Adam's blood in his veins. He was perfect.

Scripture References: Romans 5:12; I Corinthians 15:22. **Cf. Question:** 16.

Q. 35. What effect has the sin of Adam on all mankind?
A. *All mankind are born in a state of sin and misery.*

Now **ALL** mankind are born in a state of sin and misery! That means everybody! We are not born happy — we don't know what complete happiness is. There are many times in life when we experience some happiness, even when unregenerate, such as when the football team wins a game, or when we get to go swimming on a hot day, or when we have a wonderful birthday party. We may think this is the happiest moment of our lives. We also cry, and we get hurt both physically and emotionally. Awful things happen that weren't at all what we wanted to happen and they can make us miserable. There's no one who can be any more completely miserable than a child. The bottom just drops out when things don't go his way. We are born that way! Ephesians says we are born dead. Ezekiel saw the vision of the dry bones. He preached, and the Holy Spirit brought the bones to life, and they became living people. The Holy Spirit alone can regenerate dead life. The reason we are born dead is because we inherited a sinful nature, and we can only love the Lord because He first loved us and sent His Holy Spirit into our hearts to enable us to love Him, to remake or cause rebirth in that dead life. When it is reborn, then it is born a child of God and can love God. We can love the Lord only after we have been reborn. Every Christian is born twice and dies once, and every lost person is born once and dies twice. To love the Lord we have to be born twice.

Here is another important place in the catechism to present the plan of salvation (Question 35). We are all sinners but we do not have to stay in our lost condition.

Scripture References: Romans 5:12,19; Galatians 3:10.

REVIEW

By way of review, when starting a new class:
Each time the class meets, start with a review of what has been done before. If you started a new class period here, you might start your review by asking the first three questions of the catechism, and then calling the children's attention to nature around them and the beauty of the present season, and telling how the Psalmist so often mentioned that the heavens declare the glory of God and the firmament showeth His handiwork. All nature points to a creator, and in this way nature is glorifying God, for we said that glorify means to point to or make people conscious of God. Did **YOU** glorify God this week? Did you have an opportunity to stand up for the right, or to be kind to a friendless child, or in some way do something to show that you are a Christian? If not, then you have failed to be what the Lord wants you to be, and to do what the Lord wants you to do; and what kind of sin is that? Want of conformity. If you lived this week without thinking of God, including Him in your everyday occupations and thoughts and plans, then you have sinned, and what do you do? God has given us a formula to use. We are told if we will confess our sin — that means tell the Lord that we are guilty and did sin — then He will forgive our sin, and wash it away with His blood. Then we start over and we ask Him to make us stronger Christians, and ask Him to live in us a better witness. Go over and over the truths of the Scriptures because the first time the truth is presented to a child he will not get all of it. We adults know from experience that some of us heard the Gospel a long time before the magnificence of the truth ever got through to us. We

continue to present it, and the Holy Spirit alone brings the fruit in the individual's life. We are first teaching children primarily for the purpose of salvation and sanctification. We are teaching the catechism as a means to that end.

I can remember teaching the plan of salvation to a class over and over and over, realizing all the time that one little boy was not getting it at all. His expressions showed it, and his inability to say it back to me with any conviction also testified to that fact. Finally one day I asked how many in the class were saved, and this little boy's eyes lighted up, and his hand shot up. With all the conviction of a seasoned saint he gave me the plan of salvation and his assurance. Since that time he has given his testimony in youth meetings. I didn't give him that salvation. I put the facts in his mind, but only the Holy Spirit applied it to his heart. It's truly a wonderful privilege to be a teacher, because you get to plant the seed, or water the seed planted by a previous teacher; but it's God that gives the increase.

If I have not stressed this before, please allow me to stress the importance of the teacher's knowing her own salvation! If you do not know whether or not you are saved, that is the first preparation you should make before trying to help these children. By all means let's get our own salvation straight first. For it is the "joy of Thy salvation" that produces the joy and enthusiasm so important in teaching children. You must never drag to your class reluctantly! You must **ALWAYS** go to class excited and enthusiastic over the wonderful truths you have for the children; you cannot do this if you do not have it yourself.

Also in reviewing, go back and touch on another facet of a question. For example: In teaching Question 17, we touched on one part of the answer, which had to do with marriage and divorce and Eve's being formed from the body of Adam. Now in reviewing, ask Question 17, then ask, "What are *you* made out of?" Then teach the little fellows (for the big ones may already know it) that we are all made out of dust. The Bible teaches that we are made out of dust, and when we die our bodies will return to dust. The same wonderful Gospel and blessed assurance and precious hope of eternal life that are so marvelous to us are also marvelous to children, so tell them now about the resurrection of the body some day. I have known grown people who knew that the soul lives forever, but did not know that the body will rise again.

Let's have a story! Suppose you were riding a ship and fell overboard and a big fish ate you. Then commercial fishermen caught the fish, cut it up, canned the meat, and sold it for many people to eat. Then of course some day those people all die, and their bodies all turn to dust. What became of your body? How can God find your body when the day comes for all the bodies to rise again? We don't know the answer to that. All we know is that He says He can can do it and He *will* do it. The FUN part about God is that we don't know how He can do all these things, but we know He surely can do wonderful things, and He's told us some of them. He's going to raise our bodies to life again in Heaven. It is going to be me, but a new me — a glorified body that doesn't have to walk or run to get places and doesn't have scars or weaknesses. I shall be able to sing and praise God. I'm going to be better looking, and it's just going to be lots more fun living in Heaven in that new body!

Thus in review, you can touch on resurrection and eternal life in Question 17. I try always to give all the Scripture and doctrine I know — one way or another!

Now turn to page 10 of the Child's Catechism, and in reviewing Questions 23 through 26, get the children to tell the covenant of works in their own words. God and Adam made an agreement, and Adam was to mind or obey God perfectly. God said if he would, He would give to Adam eternal life, but if he did not, then God would punish him by letting him die.

Now review again Questions 28 - 30 together, calling on the children for more examples of want of conformity and transgression. Always let some child tell that sin is not being or doing what God wants you to do, and doing what God tells you not to do. When they can put it in their own words, you can know they understand it.

Review Questions 33 - 35 together. Again have the children tell in their own words that Adam and Eve were created holy and happy, but they sinned a sin of transgression (doing what God forbids) and became sinful and miserable. Adam represented (or acted for) all of us who came after him. Now all of us are born sinful and miserable. However theologically sound the song may be, this total and complete depravity of man from birth is taught in the song *"Away in a Manger."* If it is true that we are born completely self-centered, then self is on the throne from the beginning. When a baby's stomach is empty or hurts or he is uncomfortable in any way, you can stop whatever you are doing and come attend his needs! What you are doing is unimportant. All that matters is the baby's wants.

"The cattle are lowing, the poor Baby wakes,
But little Lord Jesus, no crying He makes!"

Why? Because He wasn't a sinner. If the doctrine of this song is in error, then teach it another way, but **DON'T** teach them that they are good! We must continue to teach the lost, desperate state of mankind if the doctrine of salvation is ever to get through to them. We are guilty, too often, of not teaching our children that they are really sinners. Parents, grand-parents, relatives, friends, and teachers are all guilty of teaching children that they are sweet, nice, and good. Then we have a difficult time in catechism classes getting through to them with the doctrine of total depravity. We have to undo in catechism classes what we have done to the minds of these children in everyday life. When the child begins consciously to disobey, it is time to begin telling him the precious truths of the doctrines of grace. This starts when he is very, very small, but it is necessary to get these truths to him early in life.

Q. 36. What is that sinful nature which we inherit from Adam called?
A. *Original sin.*

This question relates to Question 34, which states that Adam acted for all of us when he sinned. The first sin was Adam's sin, but since he represented us, we too are guilty. It is the same as when the President of the United States acts. He is our representative; therefore, all of us in the United States are considered as having been participants in that act. People of other nations may decide they do not like our policy, so they do not like us, and they say to us, "Yankee, go home!" We did not do anything! The president did it, but in doing it, he represented us and we are participants. All of us are guilty as citizens of this country. Likewise, we are guilty of original sin in Adam.

Scripture References: Romans 5:12,14-19.

Q. 37. What does every sin deserve?
A. The wrath and curse of God.

What does every sin deserve? "Every" is the word to be emphasized in this question. Also explain the word "deserve." It means to merit or earn. If I do wrong I deserve punishment. If I do the work in a job that I was hired to do, then I deserve or earn the pay check! If I deserve a high grade, it means that I earned it because my work was good. So every tiny little sin earns or deserves the wrath and curse of God. It is the *fair* result of the sin. Wrath means anger. God gets angry. Every sin results in God getting furious! God, the judge, is the only one who can curse anything. The reason cursing is wrong is because man is calling on God to damn something. It is really silly and pathetic to hear a person saying "damn," because he can't damn anything. Of course, we damn ourselves to condemnation through our sins. God is merely the one who pronounces the judgment. Every little sin that we commit deserves God's anger at us and condemnation of us. For example: Mother has put this big beautiful snowy white, spotlessly clean tablecloth on the table because she is having company. You have been doing homework and you accidently drop one tiny little spot of ink on the tablecloth. Does Mother get as angry about that tiny little spot as she would if you spilled a whole bottle across the middle of the cloth? Not quite, because she can cover that spot with a dish. She's angry about it, but she is not as angry as she would have been if you had ruined the whole cloth. You see, one of the meanings of the blood atonement of the Old Testament is expiation, which is a covering. "Propitiation" is a washing. Christ expiates our sins, or covers them, but He also washes them clean. That one little ink spot makes God just as angry as the whole ink bottle because it ruined the perfection of the tablecloth, and God demands perfection. He says, "Walk before me, and be thou perfect." Anything less than perfection is sin, so God has a right to be angry and condemn us to Hell for one tiny little sin. We must grasp the justice of God before we can grasp the mercy of God. We can't truly relate to the children the love of God until we first get across to them that He has this **RIGHT** to be angry at sin. It is an understanding of His justice that will give the children the proper respect and reverence and awe of God. If we don't have a God who has a perfect standard, then we have as an alternative a God who winks at sin and lets man get by with some things that are wrong. We bring God down to such a low level that He really isn't big enough to command our respect and love.

Scripture References: John 3:36; Romans 6:23; Galatians 3:10.

Q. 38. Can anyone go to Heaven with this sinful nature?
A. *No; our hearts must be changed before we can be fit for Heaven.*

No, because we have to be perfect. Our hearts are imperfect, they are sinful. Our hearts must be changed before they can be fit for Heaven. That really fixes us, doesn't it! We are in a bad shape, aren't we? Not one of us can go to Heaven and live with God because we have already done these little things that make Him angry and give Him the right to condemn us, so **NOW** what do we do? Well, what is a change of heart called? How can you change that heart? Jesus told Nicodemus you have to be born all over again. This time you are born a Christian and it's called "regeneration." Now for the seventh and eighth graders, and perhaps younger children, though not for first graders, the example of regenerating a battery is a good illustration. The car cannot run properly with a dead battery, but by being connected to the right source of power the battery is charged with life again and will operate properly. Your heart is dead in sin but, through being connected to the right power, which is God, your dead heart is raised again and now it works as a Christian. You are alive now. You are reborn. You are alive as a Christian. This also covers Question 39.

Scripture References: John 1:12-13; 3:3.

Q. 39. What is a change of heart called?
A. *Regeneration.*

Scripture Reference: Titus 3:5.

Q. 40. Who can change a sinner's heart?
A. *The Holy Spirit alone.*

This answer, I believe, is self-explanatory. Refer again to the Trinity in Question 8, and show that here we have one of the jobs, or offices, of the third person of the Trinity — to change men's hearts so they can come to Heaven and also live better lives on this earth. Time needs to be spent here helping the children understand that they are unable to change their own hearts by determining to be better. Bring in Questions 58, 59, and 71. This is a good place to emphasize man's complete helplessness and inability to save himself.

Scripture References: Matthew 19:25-26; I Corinthians 12:3; I John 3:24; I John 4:13.

If you have a child in your class about whose soul you are concerned and you are teaching these questions, please don't pass on to Question 41. Ask, "Can anyone be saved through the covenant of works?" If you have a child concerned that he is a sinner, that there is no hope for his living in Heaven with Christ, and the only thing that will get him there is for the Holy Spirit to change his heart, then his next thought is going to be, "Well, how can I get Him to do it? I want to get right with God! How do I do it?" He is not going to be the least bit concerned with the covenant of works. He will be concerned with how to get to Heaven! So turn to Question 59. Clinch the plan of salvation for that child. Tell him, "You ask God to make you a Christian. Ask Him to change your heart. How does He do it? He will accept you as His child when you accept Him as your Saviour. You tell Him you want to give your life to Him and let Him run it, and He will take over. The Holy Spirit will move into your heart and live in you. Once He comes into your heart He never leaves you." Be sure to teach the importance of repentance in this connection.

Q. 41. Can anyone be saved through the covenant of works?
A. *None can be saved through the covenant of works.*

Review Questions 23 through 26, and let the children tell you again what the covenant of works is.

Scripture References: Romans 5:12-16; Galatians 4:24-26.

Q. 42. Why can none be saved through the covenant of works?
A. *Because all have broken it, and are condemned by it.*

Remind them again of Questions 34 through 36, that all of us are born sinners because of Adam's original sin. All of us were guilty of sin long before we were even conscious of sinning. We remain guilty not only because of Adam's sin, but because of our own sin. We had all sinned before we ever heard the plan of salvation, so all are condemned, and there is the curse. Condemned. We are doomed for Hell because we have broken that covenant of works. But what do we have? We already have the promise that Christ will come into our hearts and live, so we will live in Heaven even though we've broken the covenant of works, if we accept Christ as Saviour.

Scripture References: Psalm 14:1; Romans 3:10-12; Romans 3:23.

Q. 43. With whom did God the Father make the covenant of grace?
A. *With Christ, His eternal Son.*

What is a covenant? An agreement between two or more persons. What does "eternal" mean? It means forever. God lives forever. Christ, the second person of the Trinity, lives forever. He was from the beginning. He was one of the Godhead, you remember, who was present at the creation, who made us, who is co-existent with the Father. God is one God, but in three persons (Questions 6 - 8). Two of these three persons got together up in Heaven, and planned our salvation. God the Father said, "I love her, and I want her to come to Heaven and live with us." Then Christ said, "I will die for her sins if you will let her come live with us." So they made an agreement. If you had been the only child ever to live in the whole world, you couldn't go to Heaven if they had not made this agreement and if Christ had not come to die for you! Christ didn't die because there were so *many* of us to be saved. It took Christ's blood just for *you*, to wash away *your* sins. It's true the Bible says Christ died for the sins of the world, and His blood is sufficient to wash away all the sins of the world; but it wasn't the *quantity* to be saved that caused the death — it was the sins of the individual. Your own individual sins, of which we spoke previously as looking as small as tiny ink spots to us, were sufficiently heinous to cause Christ to have to die for you. This, then, is the agreement that God the Father and God the Son made in Heaven.

Scripture References: Matthew 26:39,42,44;   John 17:4-5,12.ι
I Corinthians 15:22.

Q. 44. Whom did Christ represent in the covenant of grace?
A. *His elect people.*

What is grace? The undeserved favor of God. The generally accepted theological definition of grace is the unmerited favor of God, but our children don't hear the word "merited" quite as often as they hear "deserved" and aren't quite as familiar with it. So I prefer to teach the children that it is the undeserved favor of God. When you talk about getting something you didn't deserve, they know what you're talking about. Grace, then, means you did absolutely nothing to get the favor of God; to get His love.

Go back to Question 37. Every sin deserves the wrath and curse of God. What does "deserve" mean? To get what is coming to you, that which you rightfully earn. So grace is to get that which you did not rightfully earn — that which really is not coming to you as a matter of justice. Question 37 is based on the justice of God. Question 44 is based on the mercy of God.

Christ represented His elect people in the agreement of grace. What does "represent" mean? It means He acted for them, or stood for them. Question 34 said that Adam represented everybody who came after him. We talked about how the President represents his country when he acts. Just so did Christ represent His own people.

Now what do we mean by "elect"? The chosen. When we elect officers, we choose the public officials we want. If you were elected to a class office, you were chosen because those who chose you wanted you. Therefore Christ represented His chosen people. In Question 34 whom did Adam represent? Everybody. So everybody is a sinner through Adam. But in Question 44 whom did Christ represent? Only His chosen. So everybody is not going to be saved. Everybody on earth is a sinner but everybody on earth is not going to Heaven.

Here again, teachers, don't leave this question hanging in the child's mind. Just know that you haven't yet gotten through to all of them with the plan of salvation. Stop now, as though some child has audibly asked, "How do I get to be one of the elect?" or, "How do I get to Heaven?" Tell them again that although all of us are born sinners, deserving the wrath and curse of God (which is eternal life in Hell), still the Holy Spirit can change a *sinner's heart and make him fit for Heaven.* The way He can change it is for us to commit our lives to Him and ask Him to come into our hearts and change us and forgive us for our sins. Please tell this over and over and over. You will notice, too, that as you advance further into the catechism, you have more doctrine on which to build, so that you continue to use doctrine already taught to teach further doctrine.

Scripture References: John 6:37,44; John 15:16; John 17:2,6,9,11,14.

Now put Questions 43 through 45 together, and get the children to tell you the covenant of grace in their own words. God the Father and God the Son made an agreement, and God the Son said He would live God's law perfectly on earth in the form of a man. Then He would die for the sins of those people whom God the Father had elected and chosen and given to Him. God the Father's part of the agreement was to save them, and let them come to Heaven if Christ carried out His part of the agreement. God's part of the covenant is explained in Questions 49 through 51, so it is sufficient here just to say that He agreed to save those for whom Christ should die.

Also go back to Questions 23 through 26 and again have the children tell the covenant of works in their own words and compare it with the covenant of grace. The covenant of works was between God and man. The covenant of grace was between God the Father and God the Son. Of course, as we get into advanced theology, we learn and understand that the three persons were present in the covenant of grace, for the Holy Spirit's work was to enable the elect to accept and to work the work of sanctification in their lives, but only the two parts for the purpose of salvation are taught to the children at this age level. And man wasn't in this one at all! God didn't agree with man on anything in the covenant of grace. Man merely is the **OBJECT** of the undeserved favor of God. Adam broke the covenant of works. Did anyone break the covenant of grace? No, God is faithful. Continue in future reviews to have the children tell the covenant of works in their own words and also the covenant of grace in their own words.

Q. 45. What did Christ undertake in the covenant of grace?
A. *To keep the whole law for His people, and to suffer the punishment due to their sins.*

"Undertake" means to decide to, to take on one's self to do. *You* know this — I'm telling you what *your child* doesn't know! I want you to remain conscious of the need to explain the meaning of many, many words of the Child's Catechism. What, then, did Christ decide to do? Here we have an agreement. Christ said He would keep the whole law for His people and suffer the punishment due to their sins.

There are two parts to the covenant of grace. In Questions 24 and 26 you will see there were two parts to the covenant of works. Adam was to keep the whole law perfectly. If he didn't, he was to be punished with death. Christ fulfilled the two parts of the covenant of works. Christ kept the law perfectly. The law couldn't be thrown out or discarded because man couldn't keep it, for the law was good and perfect. God is perfect. So anything God gives is perfect. His law is perfect. Adam's breaking the law was not sufficient grounds for God to abandon that law. God's law is perfect and it stands. So Christ came and the first thing He had to do was to live the law perfectly. He calls it "fulfilling the law." The second thing He had to do was to suffer the punishment due to our sins; and what does this one tiny little spot of ink on this white tablecloth deserve? Death and Hell. Christ came to suffer death and Hell for me, so that I could go to Heaven. We are not trying to teach the child that he has committed only one or two little tiny sins, so it is not my purpose to overwork the example of the ink on the tablecloth. But very probably we will be teaching "respectable" children of church-attending families in these classes, and I have found that these children have been taught they are good and nice and sweet and fairly obedient. So it is through making them conscious of their sins, which in their eyes are small, that we teach them their need for a Saviour.

Scripture References: Matthew 26:28; Romans 5:19.

Q. 46. Did our Lord Jesus Christ ever commit the least sin?
A. *No, He was holy, harmless, and undefiled.*

Commit means do. I think this definition is necessary for the first through third grades only — I believe the rest already know this. Did Christ ever do the least little thing wrong? No. (One of our children in our catechism class answered that He was holy, harmless, and undignified!)

He was holy — what does that mean? Dedicated to God. Harmless? He never hurt anybody in any way. Undefiled means pure and perfect. Never any sin — He never did anything wrong.

Scripture References: II Corinthians 5:21; Hebrews 4:15; I Peter 2:22; I John 3:5.

Q. 47. How could the Son of God suffer?
A. *Christ, the Son of God, became man that He might obey and suffer in our nature.*

Christ became man in order to do two things as a man: obey the law perfectly, and suffer the punishment due to our sins. You see, Question 9 says God is a spirit, and has not a body like men. Then the Bible says the wages of sin is death, and without the shedding of blood there is no remission of sin; so blood has to be shed for the sin penalty. Yet a spirit doesn't have blood, so how could Christ die for me? He took on a body that could shed blood. Occasionally we still hear the old line that people killed Christ because they misunderstood Him, or for some similar reason, but that God overruled and brought good out of bad! But Christ said, "For this cause came I into the world." Christ came into the world to die for my sins. Please get this straight. I came here a sinner, and I would never get to Heaven if Christ had not come to earth to die for my sins.

Children do not believe that they have done anything bad enough for anyone to have to die for it. At the most they think their sin probably deserved a spanking or severe reprimand. Our Lord made the rules. He says, "The wages of sin is death," and, "the soul that sinneth, it shall die," and, "without the shedding of blood there is no remission for sin." When the children play a game, they play by the rules laid down by the author of the game. They do not question the rules at all, as they are part of the game. It is the same way with life. Our Lord, who gives us life, wrote the rules, and *He* says sin deserves death. We accept it because *He* says it. Our inability to understand it stems from the vast difference between our sinfulness and His holiness.

Later, in reviewing this question, ask the children if Christ could have died in the gas chamber for me today, or in the electric chair a few years ago, and paid the penalty for my sins. The answer of course is that it had to be a type of death that shed blood. This will get through particularly to the older children, and they won't forget it.

Scripture References: Philippians 2:7; Hebrews 4:15; Hebrews 9:22.

Q. 48. What is meant by the atonement?
A. *Christ's satisfying divine justice, by His sufferings and death, in the place of sinners.*

I believe this is one of the hardest questions in the catechism to teach to small children. Just do your best with it and at least some of it will get across to the little ones. I do think you can make sixth graders understand it.

"Satisfying" is the first word to consider and explain. "Satisfied" means to be completely and perfectly content. If you're satisfied, you don't want any more, and don't want the situation changed any. So Christ made God perfectly content with what He gave Him. He shed His blood to pay for my sins and God said, "That's enough. That's all I want for Joyce's sins. I want your blood. You paid it. Now she can come to Heaven and live with us. That's all it takes. **IF SHE BELIEVES IT** that's all it takes." Christ satisfied God's justice and that is what "divine" means. We're not divine. If you're a Christian, you strive to be holy, but "holy" means dedicated to God. "Divine" refers to the nature of God Himself.

Christ pleased, suited, satisfied God's justice.

What is justice? In courts we have trials to see that a person gets what is due him, or what is coming to him. If he has done wrong and deserves punishment, he gets this through a trial. If he is innocent and should go free, we have courts to see that he gets what he deserves. In other words, justice is just fairness. We have courts and laws so that we will deal fairly and justly with one another. God, too, wants things fair. God made certain laws, and it is only fair and just that His laws be carried out. It wouldn't be fair to God if man could overrule His laws or demands, so Christ satisfied God's fairness.

How did He do it? By His sufferings and death, in the place of sinners. He did it for the sinner. Don't **EVER** forget that He loved you **SO MUCH** that He made this covenant with Christ His Son. But God is also **PERFECT**, and His fairness has to be satisfied. Therefore God Himself satisfied His own justice, because Christ was God, and He came Himself and met His own requirements for the forgiveness of our sins.

To satisfy divine justice is to satisfy God's sense of fairness. If you were playing a game with someone who cheated and did not play fair, you would become very dissatisfied, and perhaps angry, because of the way he was cheating. If someone else came along and took his place in the game and played fairly, then your sense of justice or fairness would be satisfied, and you would no longer be angry or upset. God had a right to be angry with us and the way we act, but Christ satisfied God's sense of fairness by dying in our place, by dying the death we deserved to die for our sins. The best you can do with this is just play it over and over. I believe some of it gets through to the child.

Scripture References: Romans 5:10; I Corinthians 15:3; II Corinthians 5:21; I Peter 3:18.

Q. 49. What did God the Father undertake in the covenant of grace?
A. *To justify and sanctify those for whom Christ should die.*

This question means, "What did God the Father determine to do, or decide to do, in the agreement with His Son, about the undeserved favor of God toward sinful man?" "Undertake" means take upon one's self the responsibility of doing. What is grace? The undeserved favor of God. Go over that definition as often as you do the definition of holy. Be sure your children know what those two words mean. The covenant of grace is the agreement between the Father and the Son, that "we'll do something for those sinners they don't deserve." What did Christ the Son say He'd do? He'd keep the law, and suffer the punishment due to our sins. He'd die for us, and He'd live a perfect life for us. God the Father said, "If you'll do your part, I'll bring them, these sinners, to Heaven. I'll justify them and I'll sanctify them."

Now connect 50 and 51 with Question 41, because the words justify and sanctify aren't going to mean anything to these children. God the Father said, "I'll justify and sanctify all those for whom Christ should die." And for whom did Christ die? His elect people.

Scripture References: Romans 8:30; I Corinthians 1:30.
Cf. Questions: 43-45.

Q. 50. What is justification?
A. *It is God's forgiving sinners and treating them as if they had never sinned.*

That makes God better than your mother, because when a child breaks a treasured object of mother's, she will forgive him. She still misses the treasure, perhaps grieves over it, and sometimes it takes her a while to get over it and consider it unimportant. But you know, God *forgets* it! Do you know how He does it? Christ takes our sins and hides them from God. Do you know how far He hides them? As far as the East is from the West. God remembers them no more against us because Christ hid them under His blood. We can sin right this minute, in our thoughts alone, and the very next second confess it to God and He forgives it and forgets it. Then He treats us as if we had never sinned! That's a marvelous blessing! Every minute the Christian can start a fresh page because God forgives us and treats us as if we had never sinned.

Scripture References: Romans 5:1; Titus 3:4-7.

Q. 51. What is sanctification?
A. *It is God's making sinners holy in heart and conduct.*

What is "holy?" It is pure, completely dedicated to God. What is "holy in heart"? It is being pure and clean and good in your thoughts, in what you think about. What is "conduct?" That is how we act, what we do, how we behave. When we become Christians, God, in the person of the Holy Spirit, works continually in our lives to turn us more and more away from sin and toward purity and goodness. He does this by giving us, in His Word, directions for the way He wants us to live, and then by enabling us from within to conform to His standards. As we think about good, pure, true things, He purifies our minds. As we delight to be kind, tender-hearted, forgiving, unselfish, etc., He purifies our conduct. Justification is an act of God's free grace. It is accomplished instantaneously. Sanctification is a *work* of God's free grace; it goes on the remainder of our lives on this earth. We become children of God instantly, but we do not become mature Christians instantly. That is a process of growth, whereby He empowers us and enables us to live more and more for Him, and to turn more and more away from sin.

Scripture References: Ephesians 1:4; II Thessalonians 2:13.

REVIEW

After 50 or 51 questions, it is a good time to review.
After studying sanctification, go back to Question 3 and let them tell you if they are now conscious of efforts on their behalf to live more to God's glory, or to live more and more unto righteousness and die more and more unto sin. Every age should be able to give

specific examples, or at least think of private ones, where their lives have in these past few weeks shown definite spiritual growth as they center their minds more on Christ and try to live to God's glory.

Go over the covenant of works again, having the group tell it in their own words. They will be memorizing the catechism in the exact wording, but to satisfy yourself that they understand it, require them to give it back to you in their own words. The covenant of works is found in Questions 23-26.

Then take Questions 28-30 and have them give the definition of sin, want of conformity, and transgression in catechism language, then also in their own language. Be sure they understand that sin is any lack of being or doing what God wants you to be or do, and also doing what God doesn't want you to do.

Every sin deserves the wrath and curse of God. Wrath is anger, and curse is condemnation. Did Christ ever really curse anything? Yes, He cursed the fig tree. Why? Because it didn't bear fruit. Now here we are to sanctification again. Christ didn't curse the fig tree because it didn't do enough work to find grace in His eyes, but He cursed the fig tree because its failure to bear fruit was an outward evidence of the trouble which was inward. It was a picture for us today. If we are truly saved through repentance and commitment, then our lives must surely show it. When they don't we are in danger of Hell, not because of a lack of sufficient works, but because the lack of works or fruits was a result of not having Christ in our hearts, and it is being without Christ that condemns. Christ doesn't condemn us to Hell because we don't do good works, but we are condemned to Hell if we don't do good works because those good works are a definite proof of our salvation. The Bible says if we're saved we'll show it with our works. It's one of those assurances we've been given, that now if I *want* to serve the Lord and glorify Him, this is a fruit of the Spirit. Maybe I have a terrible temper, and I want to control that temper for the glory of God because I'm a Christian. It may be a long time before anyone can see any improvement in my temper, but you won't be able to know the heartache that goes on inside me, and the prayer sessions that are a result of my succumbing to that sin of temper. You see I'm wrestling with the Lord now over temper often. And that is the fruit, the result. The fruits are the results of being a Christian. So we're not condemned because we don't show fruit as a work, but the thing that condemns us is the fact that there was no real salvation. If we are reborn, we are going to bear fruit. John 15 tells us that. So as you keep going back, keep giving them more theology, because as they get salvation the next thing is to get assurance. When you lead these children to the Lord, then edify them (as taught us in the fourth chapter of Ephesians).

Now tell them about the covenant of grace, Questions 43-45, and let them tell it in their own words. Grace is the undeserved favor of God. That is what saves us! This was an agreement between God the Father and God the Son: God the Father said He would forgive sinners and treat them as if they had never sinned, and He would make them dedicated to Him in what they think and how they act. That was His part of the agreement. Christ's part of the agreement was that He would obey the law perfectly, and He would suffer the punishment due to our sins. The children need to go *over and over that to get it.*

Q. 52. For whom did Christ obey and suffer?
A. *For those whom the Father had given Him.*

Your Scriptural references are really important here because you're getting into the doctrine of election. If there's anything any harder to understand than predestination, it's election! It is hard for us to realize that we didn't choose Christ, but He chose us. This is what is said in John 15:16 and in Christ's high priestly prayer in John 17. He prays for those whom the Father hath given Him. Now go back and review again Question 34, only ask it in your own words, for here you are teaching the theology rather than the verbatim memory work. Whom did Adam represent in the covenant of works? He represented all his posterity. He represented or acted for everyone! Now, Question 44: Whom did Christ represent in the covenant of grace? His elect people. For whom did Christ obey and suffer? Those whom the Father had given Him. Whom had the Father given Him? The elect people, those chosen by God to be saved. I believe the Scriptural references in John will clear up this point. It is always a shock to men to learn they aren't saved because they came to Christ but because Christ chose them and gave them the ability to come to Him!

Go to Question 58. Can you repent and believe in Christ by your own power? No, I can do nothing good without the help of God's Holy Spirit. The Scriptures teach us that the natural man is at enmity with God — there is nothing about God that any should desire Him. Left to ourselves we would **NEVER** turn to God because men love darkness rather than light.

We see this in Genesis, in the Garden of Eden. When man sinned he didn't run to God for forgiveness, he ran from God and left to himself he would have remained away from God. It is God who does the reconciling between Himself and sinful man. It is God who reaches out to us. We love Him **BECAUSE** He first loved us! This problem will not give any trouble to those in the second through about the sixth grades. It is only as we begin to get older that it begins to bother us. It will not be necessary to explain to the little ones, but it may need to be explained to older groups (from 7th grade up).

I think a good illustration of God's privilege of choosing, is that of the governor, who has the privilege of pardoning a penitentiary inmate. The prisoner is there because he did wrong and deserves to suffer the penalty. But because the governor is governor, he has the privilege of pardoning one and setting him free — not because he is innocent, for all the world knows he is guilty, but only because the governor chooses to do so! No one denies the governor this power, or right; neither does anyone deny the fact that all the prisoners are suffering their just dues. When we get bogged down with election and fail to understand it, if we'll just look first at ourselves as sinners, remembering that all of us have sinned and are guilty and deserve the wrath of God and the punishment due to our sin, then it will not be so difficult for us to grant to God the privilege of pardoning a guilty sinner if He so chooses. At the same time we cannot stand in judgment of God and say that because he pardoned

John Doe, He **OWES** it to Bill Smith to pardon him also! None of us says that because the governor chose one prisoner he should free them all. Therefore, if God looks down and sees that we are bad, all doomed to Hell, and He decides He wants some of us to come live in Heaven with Him, and He pays the price to get us there, that is His privilege!

Scripture References: John 6:37; 10:26-28; 15:16; 17:9,11,12.

Q. 53. What kind of life did Christ live on earth?
A. *A life of poverty and suffering.*

What is poverty? That's certainly something that needs to be explained to the average child today because they don't know it and haven't experienced it. Poverty is being very poor. Christ was born to poor parents and even when grown He said, "Foxes have holes and birds have nests but the Son of man hath not where to lay His head." The Scriptural references on this one are so interesting that I would let the children look them up for themselves. In Leviticus 12:1-8, and 5:7, is the law that a person is to bring a lamb for the offering to be sacrificed, but if he is poor and cannot afford to bring a lamb, either from his own flock or by buying one, he is to offer two turtledoves, which were free. Then turn to Luke 2:24-25, and you will see that when Joseph and Mary brought Jesus to the temple for dedication, they brought for their offering two turtledoves! This was the offering of very poor people. I'd let every child every age look up these references, for it will impress it upon their minds and they'll understand.

Christ did live a life of poverty, but why do you think the catechism says He lived a life of suffering? We know He died a death of suffering, but did He live that kind of life? We don't have any references to His having any terrible accidents, or having to have surgery, or any serious diseases. As far as we know, we don't think He suffered on earth. The suffering that Christ endured, that we ourselves need to understand, and need to get through to our children, is the fact that He became man! He had to suffer the humiliation of coming to earth as a baby, and let Mary dress Him and tend to Him and feed Him and take care of Him as a helpless baby — and this was God Himself! This was the very God that made the earth and created Mary and created Joseph! Luke 2:51 tells us that He, who had sat in the temple confounding the doctors at twelve years of age with His knowledge and ability, He who knew that Mary and Joseph were sinners and that He must die for their salvation — this very God was **SUBJECT** to them. He allowed these two sinners to have authority over Him, telling Him what to do and where He could go, etc. Thus God Himself so humbled Himself that He limited Himself to the limitations of man — hunger, thirst, travel, heat and cold — all the discomforts and displeasures and inconveniences of humanity, to save us. We never stop to realize that to be a man had to be a humbling experience for God. We take these inconveniences and discomforts for granted because this is the only life we've known. But Christ had to walk somewhere that He could have just appeared. He walked for miles, one step at a time. And He worked. The God who created the universe by the word of His power could not make anything on earth without doing it the way man would do it. This is a sample of the suffering He experienced. We think it's pretty nice to be a human. What if you had to be a donkey or a camel or something bungling and dumb and not as smart as you are? We don't stop to realize what a tremendous step down it was for Christ to become a man, because we don't realize that He is as much higher over us as we are over an animal. This may be a poor illustration, but let's realize that it wasn't a small, inconsequential act for God to become man. It was an act of humility and suffering.

Scripture References: Leviticus 5:7; Leviticus 12:1-8; Matthew 8:20; Luke 2:24,25,51.

Q. 54. What kind of death did Christ die?
A. *The painful and shameful death of the cross.*

This should be impressed upon these children — every age, as much as is possible for the teacher to do. I would take every narration of the death on the cross, from each of the four Gospels, and read them. Give to the children a graphic picture of what actually happened, and get them to underline in their Bibles every thing that happened to Christ at His death. They put a crown of thorns on His head, and then they beat it in with sticks. We don't stop to think about that! They mocked Him and they spit upon Him. I was telling this to a class of 7th graders and they seemed to think it was pretty awful but quite familiar, until I talked about their spitting on Him and the spittle running down His face. One little boy became absolutely furious and said, "Now I wouldn't have taken that!" You never know what part of Christ's suffering will impress each child the most. And He did it for them! They stripped Him. (What can be more embarrassing for anyone to suffer than nakedness?) They put a purple robe on Him and mocked Him. (What physical suffering is much greater than intense ridicule?) They bound His hands. They tied them so when they spit on Him He couldn't wipe it off. When they tormented Him, He wouldn't defend Himself. And all of this He suffered for my sins! I think it needs to be emphasized! I would take each chapter and list the sufferings Christ endured for us. You know, sometimes a person would hang on the cross for five or six days before dying. It was a horrible death, reserved for the very worst of criminals for it was slow and torturous. You can imagine exactly what happened — the pain on the hands would be so intense that a person would brace with his feet against the upright bar to take some of the strain off the hands and give them relief — until the feet began to hurt so badly that they'd sag to take the weight off the feet, and it would tear the hands again as the weight of the body hung by the hands. Often gangrene would set in, and flies and insects would worry the wounds.

This particular crucifixion was on the day before the Sabbath day, and the law forbade anyone's hanging on the cross during the Sabbath day, so they'd hasten the death by breaking their legs. That would prevent their bracing their weight on their feet, and thus the breath would be cut off and result in death more quickly. So they broke the bones of the two thieves, but when they came to Christ He was dead already. You remember how they marveled that anyone could die so quickly on the cross! But back in Exodus, when they were to kill the Passover lamb, they were to roast him whole, "not a bone was to be broken." And John tells us that not a bone of Christ was broken, "that the scripture might be fulfilled!" He gave up His spirit when He was through suffering the wrath and curse of God for us, but He first hung there in agony and pain for six hours for you and me.

I do not believe it necessary to protect little children from the blood sacrifice of our Saviour (which was a complete fulfillment of the blood sacrifices of the Old Testament) because our Christian doctrine is built on faith in the shed blood of Christ. If no one else had ever lived on this earth but me, it would have been necessary for Christ to have suffered all these horrible atrocities for me. It was necessary for Him to suffer it for each one of these children whom we are teaching, and I think they ought to know it.

Crucifixion was also a shameful death. Explain that "shameful" is embarrassing and humiliating. The central place is always the place of highest position. If the governor is with us at a feast, he does not sit at the end of the table, but in the center. Those of lesser importance are seated at the ends. The Gospels tell us that when Christ was crucified, He was hanging in the center, between the two thieves — the place signifying the **WORST** of the three. This was a shameful death for Christ, and all the mockery He endured was shameful.

Also, crucifixion was not the only Roman way of execution, but it was the lowest or basest, reserved for the worst or vilest of criminals. It was comparable to a practice in Africa prevalent today. A missionary told me recently that they also execute their criminals. But if a person has committed a crime more offensive in the eyes of the natives than other crimes, or if they hate him and his crime enough, they eat the body. This is a way of adding shame or insult to the dead criminal. It is not enough to kill him, for this only makes him on a par with other criminals. It is a way of adding insult to injury. Many criminals were killed by the Romans by other means of capital punishment, but the death reserved for the worst criminals was crucifixion. In this way the person killed was not dead in a short time but hung before the public a long time, to be ridiculed and seen by all who passed by. The Bible tells us that even those that passed by mocked at Jesus. There was no privacy or sanctity in this type of death. All this contributed to the shame of the death Christ suffered.

Scripture References: Matthew 27; Mark 15; Luke 23; John 19; Philippians 2:8; Hebrews 12:2.

Q. 55. Who will be saved?
A. *Only those who repent of sin, believe in Christ, and lead holy lives.*

Questions 55, 56, and 57 can be taught and explained together, because Question 56 explains what it means to repent, and Question 57 explains what it is to believe in Christ.

To repent is to be sorry for sin and to stop it because it grieves God and is not pleasing to Him. To believe in Christ is to believe what the Bible says about Christ's having to pay the wages of sin for us to be saved and to enter heaven.

The third part of Question 55 includes "and lead holy lives." And what kind of lives are those? Lives dedicated to God. Does this mean that if I try to live a good life I will be saved? Is equal importance placed on repentance of sin, belief in Christ, and trying to be a good person? No, the being a good person or endeavoring to live the Christian principles is the result or fruit of the other two (which are repentance and belief in Christ). Leading a holy life is our proof of whether or not our ingrafting into Christ is genuine. God was gracious enough to give us a test to prove to ourselves the genuineness of our salvation. How do I **KNOW** I'm saved? Because now I want to live as God wants me to live. My first assurance comes from the truthfulness and dependability of God's word. He **SAID** if I'd believe in Christ for salvation I'd be saved, and I took Him at His word. So I know I'll have eternal life because He promised it. But He gave us a second means of assurance also, a sure evidence of whether we are saved. He says, "You'll act differently. You'll begin to want to live better." So we start, in our lives, to dedicate our daily routines and thoughts and actions to God. That is why we are not allowed the privilege of judging each other — because I don't know what area of your life is giving you the most trouble, and how much time is spent in prayer or mourning, as you wrestle with a part of your life that must be changed.

There is a fine line between the Arminian tendency in most of us to *try* to be "good," and the desire for holiness which is a result of the salvation wrought in us by the Lord. Time should be spent with the children explaining the difference as best we can. Leading holy lives does not *result* in salvation. We repent of our sins, believe in Jesus Christ alone for salvation, and within us is born that desire to crucify the flesh and its desires, and to lead a new life glorifying God. Parents have been guilty of a pragmatic approach to moral living, by teaching the child that other children will like them better if they'll share, etc. The *only* reason we share that which we consider our own is because God our Father requires it in His Word, and the Holy Spirit within us desires to be obedient to the Word. It is not for what good it will get us! It is purely to glorify our Lord! We are not only battling a pragmatism instilled by parents, but also taught generally by teachers, friends, family, and society.

Scripture References: Acts 16:31; James 2:17.

Q. 56. What is it to repent?
A. *To be sorry for sin, and to hate and forsake it, because it is displeasing to God.*

When you do wrong and are sorry for it, why are you sorry? Because Mother caught you and punished you? Or because Daddy showed his disappointment in you? Or because the teacher caught you and embarrassed you before the class? Or because your friends turned their backs on you? True repentance means you are sorry because God didn't like it. If we stop doing wrong for **ANY OTHER REASON** we haven't truly repented. We have just stepped a step higher on the moral ladder, but we haven't repented. We may turn over a new leaf, or give up a habit because it isn't socially accepted or is harmful to our health — but this is not repentance. Explain "forsake" to the little fellows, because "forsake" means to stop or quit; and explain "displeasing" to them, for they may not know that "displeasing" means it doesn't make God happy. When we are unhappy over something, we are displeased. HOW sorry are we that we did wrong? Sorry enough to quit it! To be embarrassed or a little ashamed because we did a wrong thing, but then to sneak to do it again is not repentance. Being sorry for every time we willfully do it is not true repentance. In salvation, repentance means being sorry for all our sins, our sinful condition, and our individual sins; in sanctification, repentance includes being so sorry for specific sins that we turn away from them, and stop them, because they are an offense to God. Children are as bad as adults, or worse, at being able blithely to confess themselves as sinners, and unable to face, admit, and deal with specific sins in the individual's life. They tend to name sins in the other fellow, rather than those of which they themselves are guilty. To be able to help the children see themselves as dirty sinners is to be able to help them see their real need of a Saviour.

Scripture References: Job 42:6; Psalm 5:5; Psalm 97:10; Isaiah 55:7; Revelation 2:15-16.

Q. 57. What is it to believe or have faith in Christ?
A. _To trust in Christ alone for salvation._

We have many references, of course, all through Scripture, teaching us that faith in Christ alone saves us. "Salvation" means being saved. Saved from what? From life in Hell. Saved to what? To eternal life in Heaven with our triune God. But it also means saved from the power of sin in our lives today, not _just_ Heaven at death, but victory now, today.

This is an important place to stop and again explain the plan of salvation simply and thoroughly to the class. They should be made fully aware (all ages) that once you are born into this world, you can never become extinct — you **MUST** live forever, somewhere! There are only two alternatives, but for sure you'll be in one place or the other. We cannot over-emphasize the importance of trust in Christ alone for salvation. This is a good time for testimonies. Here I ask if anyone in class knows positively that he or she is going to Heaven. If so, I get that one to tell the others how to have salvation and assurance. This strengthens the faith of the one witnessing and also that of the ones listening.

Now review Questions 55, 56, and 57 together so the children can give them in their own words and also in the words of the catechism, and so you yourself will know that they understand them. Even second-graders should be able to understand this simple presentation of the plan of salvation.

In going over Questions 55 and 56, be sure the children understand that it is not necessary for them to **UNDERSTAND WHY** God doesn't like a certain thing, or for them to **AGREE WITH HIM** that it is wrong. There are some things the Bible forbids for which I can see absolutely no reason, but I am not the judge of sin — God is. When I find something the Bible says for me to refrain from doing, and I love doing it, I must be sorry I am doing it and **STOP IT, BECAUSE** God doesn't like that. That is the only reason for stopping, and that must be thoroughly drilled into children. It comes as a shock that sin is something we can enjoy!

However, the other side of the coin is also true; that even when we do *not* like what we are doing, we are *slaves* to sin, and can't stop it unless we are born again and given the power of the Holy Spirit to overcome it.

Scripture References: John 3:16; John 10:9; John 14:6.

Q. 58. Can you repent and believe in Christ by your own power?
A. No; I can do nothing good without the help of God's Holy Spirit.

Now, review Question 40: Who can change a sinner's heart? The Holy Spirit alone. That's the job, or work, of the Holy Spirit. Where is God the Father? He's seated in Heaven. Where is God the Son? He's seated at the right hand of God the Father, interceding, or praying, for the saints, or the Christians. Where is God the Holy Spirit? He's down here in the hearts of Christians. The Bible tells us that everyone who is born again has the Holy Spirit within him, and He is teaching us all things, and enabling us to live holy lives. He is the one who enables us to trust Christ.

If that confuses you, remember there is nothing about God that any human being would desire Him. The natural man is at enmity with God. I would never come to Christ without the Holy Spirit's first working in my heart, for I would prefer the things of this world — "for men love darkness rather than light". Man would never turn from sin in his own strength and decide to turn to Christ. God, because He chose me, sent the Holy Spirit into my heart and enabled me to accept, so that conversion followed regeneration. Regeneration was the Holy Spirit's coming into my heart and immediately enabling me to commit my life to Christ. That was my conversion. I could do nothing good without the help of the Holy Spirit, not even trust Christ. Give more emphasis to this matter, because although most of us admit that we don't believe in works salvation, we still have a tendency to say, "I'm going to Heaven because I accepted Christ." That is actually something you did, and that doesn't give God the glory for the conversion. *He* is the one who saves us! When giving their personal testimony, people do not say, "I know I'm going to Heaven because I heard the Gospel story and believed it and repented and accepted — ," they say, "I'm going to Heaven because God saved me."

Now if you have taught this class thus far with much prayer about the soul salvation of the individual members of your class, you should be able to seal some person's salvation with Question 59, if the Holy Spirit so pleases.

Scripture References: John 3:3-5; John 3:27; John 6:65; John 15:5; Acts 16:14; I Corinthians 12:3.

Q. 59. How can you get the help of the Holy Spirit?
A. *God has told us that we must pray to Him for the Holy Spirit.*

I learn that I am a sinner. (Questions 35-40), that I cannot get to Heaven with this sinful nature, that Christ died only for His elect people, and that only those who repent of sin, believe in Christ, and lead holy lives can get to Heaven and that I cannot do any of these things without the help of the **HOLY SPIRIT**. This should lead inevitably to the next question: "Then how **CAN** I get the help of the Holy Spirit?" The very heart-searching question to which we want to bring these children is: "How can I be saved?" So they should be asking very sincerely now, "How can I get the help of the Holy Spirit?" "When do I get it?" "How does it come?" God has told us that we must pray to Him for the Holy Spirit. It's as simple as that. Now it sounds like a contradiction, because we have just taught that "I can do nothing good without the help of God's Holy Spirit," so how can I pray to God for the help of the Holy Spirit without already having the Holy Spirit enabling me to do the praying? But the very fact that I want the help of the Holy Spirit is evidence that He is already working in my heart enabling me to desire the things of God, to desire salvation. But God says we must ask to receive, therefore He sends His Holy Spirit to enable us to ask Him to send His Holy Spirit! Perhaps Isaiah 56:24 will help clarify this, for in this verse the Lord promises, "Before they call, I will answer: and while they are yet speaking I will hear."

Now it will also help us to look at the fact that there are two calls of the Gospel: the external call, which is the preaching of the Gospel, or the telling of the story of salvation, and the internal call, which is the Holy Spirit's working within the heart of the individual to enable him to receive the gift of faith. We can issue the external call, and are commanded to do so. All of us have probably had experiences of wanting to win some loved one to Christ, and telling that person the Gospel, and giving our personal testimony of what Christ means to us. But we cannot save that person; the Holy Spirit has to work within his heart. So God has taught us that we must pray to Him for the Holy Spirit. What we mean, then, by the effectual calling, is the Holy Spirit's working within hearts to make the external call effective. If we have a person who has been brought to Question 59, sincerely asking how to get the Holy Spirit, then we as Christian teachers recognize that the Holy Spirit is already working in that heart. Our answer is for that person to do what? To pray! Ask! This is necessary for salvation.

After Question 59 is a good place to review Questions 27, 34-36, and 41-42. All these are questions that will convince each one of sin. Then review 37, what sin deserves, then 43-45, the covenant of grace, and 49-52 together, letting them give you again the covenant of grace in their words. Next 38-40 teach regeneration, and 55-58 will bring you to how you can get this regeneration. Any person ought to be able to lead a child, a first-grader, to Christ, with the first 60 questions of the catechism, if the Holy Spirit so wills.

Scripture Reference: Luke 11:13.

Q. 60. How long ago is it since Christ died?
A. *More than nineteen hundred years.*

This is a question so exciting and wonderful that I have never felt that I could find appropriate words to teach it adequately! And it looks like one of the dullest ones. How many years is it since Christ died? One thousand, nine hundred, and seventy-six. What would you say everyone considers the most important thing that ever happened in history? That includes Charlemagne's reign, the Napoleonic reign, the time of the Caesars (when Rome governed the whole of the Mediterranean empire) — what would you say is recognized as the most important thing that ever happened? It is the birth and death of Christ, the coming of the Saviour, the one whom the Jews of the Old Testament prophesied would come. Even people who claim to be atheists date all of their papers, letters, receipts, etc., every day, May 4, 1976, anno dominie — and what does that mean? "In the year of our Lord." Anno dominie means in the year of our Lord! Isn't that perfectly thrilling! It is a marvelous fact for these children to discover that the whole world revolves around the dating set around the death of Christ, the year of our Lord. It's really one of the jokes that Christians have on the non-Christians — the people who, in superior knowledge and sophistication, say there is no God, and then write on their checks,

"In the year of our Lord, 1976." If he doesn't believe in God, he has no date! There's no way for him to say what day it is, and so it turns out to be a joke on him, and it's one the children will thoroughly enjoy discovering. Don't skim or minimize Question 60. When a child can comprehend the fact that the coming of Christ our Saviour is so important that all history is dated as being before or after that time, it is a marvelous revelation to him. He will enjoy thinking about the fact that every time we date something, we are giving glory to God. The non-Christian who doesn't want to give God the glory can think and try and work at it, but he simply cannot tell you something happened unless he finally uses the dating system that has already been set up, which revolves around Christ. I would suggest that you bring a diploma, or some such impressive paper to class that has the words "in the year of our Lord" written on it, for it likely will be the first time the children have been faced with that.

Reference: The calendar!

Q. 61. How were pious persons saved before the coming of Christ?
A. *By believing in a Saviour to come.*

Explain the word "pious" to your little ones. It would be a good idea to explain it to all, to be sure they understand it. The pious are people who, through repentance of their sins and belief in an atonement or a salvation through a substitute, are endeavoring to lead holy lives, and have triumphed in their faith to the extent that some of the fruit is beginning to show. Some of their light is beginning to shine. For us today the word pious means they not only have faith, but are showing the fruit of their faith. To be perfectly correct I'm sure that the word here in the context of this question means simply the saved, those who have saving faith. The seventh and eighth graders may have an incorrect idea of pious that will need correcting (that it's a meek, mousey, super-good, holier-than-thou kind of person that they won't like). For that matter, meek is also a good word, but you'd never find an eighth-grade boy anywhere who wants to be meek! Yet Moses was the meekest man on the face of the earth, and one of God's greatest servants because meek means disciplined by God. It means **COMPLETELY** surrendered to the will of God, and the more surrendered a person is, the bigger he is. Christ said, "I am meek and lowly in heart," and Christ was completely surrendered to the will of God. So pious and meek are both good words which need to be elevated to their proper status in a child's vocabulary.

Questions 61, 62, and 63 together ought to constitute one whole class period.

All of those persons in the Old Testament who never saw Christ and never had the complete Gospel that we have were saved by belief in a saviour to come. When was that coming saviour first promised? This is an interesting part. The prophets said there was a saviour coming. He was **FIRST** promised in Genesis 3:15. And to whom was He promised? Who was the first person the Lord told that a Saviour was coming to save the Christians? Satan! Isn't that interesting? God told the man what his punishment would be. He told the woman what her punishment would be, and He told Satan what his punishment would be. And Satan's punishment was that the Christ would come and defeat him.

"I will put enmity between thee and the woman, and between thy seed and her seed; it shall bruise thy head, and thou shall bruise his heel." Humans are known as the seed of the man. The man is the one who plants the seed propagating the human race. So when he says the seed of a woman, He told Satan the Christ would be virgin born. When He says, "Thou shalt bruise his heel," He told him it would be a man. It's wonderful! In Exodus at the Passover the lamb which was to be perfect and without blemish was to be a male lamb. He would be killed at the prime of his life when he was worth the most, and it was at 33 that Christ died, considered the prime of human life. (Before that we're considered not really mature, and after that we're older and past our prime. Thirty-three is still considered about the peak of life.) Everything about the Passover told what kind of Messiah He'd be. Pious people were saved by believing in a saviour to come.

Who do you think were the first people to believe in a saviour to come? Were Adam and Eve saved? We believe they were saved by believing in a saviour to come because they named their first child "Cain," which means "a man given of God." They apparently thought he was the Messiah. They knew they couldn't be saved unless God sent a man as saviour of the world, and they thought Cain was the Messiah, so they named him "a man given of God," which is a little hint to us that Adam and Eve believed in a saviour to come.

Scripture References: Galatians 3:7-9; Hebrews 11:3.

Q. 62. How did they show their faith?
A. *By offering sacrifices on God's altar.*

We know that the Lord Himself required the shedding of blood as payment of sin, for He says, "Without the shedding of blood there is no remission for sin," and He proved it in Genesis when Adam and Eve had sinned and had covered their nakedness with fig leaves. The Lord killed an animal because blood had to be shed for their sin. He clothed them with the skin, but I doubt if their bodies were covered with the skin any more than they had been with the fig leaves. The leaves may have covered more of their nakedness, but they could not cover the sin. There we find the fig a picture of work, of man's effort to save himself from his own sin. Now we understand better why Christ cursed the fig tree in the New Testament, so that it would never bear fruit again. The Lord killed the animal, clothed them with the skin of the animal, and thus covered their sins sufficiently through the shed blood of the animal. It was this that got through to Abel, and he understood that his belief in a saviour to come could only be manifest through a sacrifice of shed blood. But Cain did not believe, and he offered the works of his hands, which was not shed blood, so his sacrifice was not accepted. It was not pleasing to the Lord. Cain's heart was not right, consequently he couldn't bring an acceptable offering.

Scripture Reference: Hebrews 10:1.

Q. 63. What did these sacrifices represent?
A. *Christ, the Lamb of God, who was to die for sinners.*

"What did these sacrifices represent?" Explain the word represent to the little ones. It means "stand for." What did they stand for?

You just must stop and read John 1:29. When John saw Christ coming out of the wilderness, he said, "Behold, the Lamb of God that taketh away the sins of the world." All those years in the Old Testament they had sacrificed lambs, bulls, turtle doves, and all manner of sacrifices, but the *lamb* was the *Passover* offering. This was, then, the Lamb of God. John meant — "Here comes the perfect sacrifice, the sacrifice to end all sacrifices." They had to bring their own lamb, you know, for sacrifice. It had to be out of their own flock, and that's what started all that trading in the Temple. If they didn't own one, they had to buy one. They couldn't borrow a neighbor's; they had to sacrifice their own lamb. So when John said, "The Lamb of God," he meant, "Here comes God's own sacrifice; He's going to sacrifice His lamb and that's going to take away the sins of the world."

The Lord says, "Do you think I'll be satisfied with the blood of bulls and rams? If I were hungry, I wouldn't ask you. I own the cattle on a thousand hills. I don't need your sacrifices." But He had His own sacrifice. These sacrifices were types that showed the faith of the person in the Old Testament who looked *toward* the cross — the faith in a saviour to come. What saves us is looking *back* at the very same cross. Our belief is in a *Saviour who did come.* Their belief was in the same *Saviour who was to come.*

(If you have time here, explain the rent veil. You may prefer to wait until you get into Christ's being a priest.) The Lord was the first priest because He was the first to kill an animal for the sins of His people, and He covered Adam and Eve with the skins. When Christ died on the cross, the curtain was rent from top to bottom in the Tabernacle. There was a curtain nobody could go behind but the high priest, because the Ark of the Covenant was back there, which represented the presence of God. Nobody could go back there and live. The High Priest couldn't touch the Ark and live. He had bells around the bottom of his robe and as long as he moved around in there, sprinkling the blood from the animals on the four corners, they could hear his bells and they knew he was alive. But if he accidentally touched the Ark, if he in any way offered the worship to God in a way displeasing to God and was struck dead, his bells would quit ringing, and they would know something had happened to their High Priest. (So it was a fearful thing to fall into the hand of the living God, and it still is. We all need a High Priest. We'd never make it going straight to God ourselves.) They went through a High Priest. Then Christ hung on the cross and died at three o'clock in the afternoon. There in the edge of town was a Jewish rabbi still offering sacrifices, and the temple curtain was torn from the top to show that God tore it. He says you no longer go through a *human* High Priest, now you go through "my son" as High Priest.

That's why we teach the children to pray in Christ's name. We don't just pray to the Lord and tell Him what we want, and ask Him for forgiveness, etc., and then say "Amen." We'd never make it, because we're sinful and our prayers are sinful. But our High Priest takes our prayers and mingles His own with them, and presents them perfect before the throne. Therefore we teach our children to say, "for Christ's sake," "in Christ's name I pray."

I think I was in high school when I decided I was big enough not to say that. It sounded childish. I thought that was something Mother taught me with "Now I lay me down to sleep," so when I was "grown" I didn't say "for Christ's sake." But I only did it once! My mother straightened me out the first time I left it off. I just thought I had out-grown it, that it was for the little ones. But those are the only prayers heard, the ones prayed in the name of Christ. This leads you right into Questions 64 and 65 on the offices of Christ.

Scripture References: I Peter 1:9; John 1:29,36.

Q. 64. What offices has Christ?
A. Christ has three offices.

Explain "offices" to them. It means jobs or positions; otherwise, they may think He has a whole floor of offices in an office building. You don't know what some little first-grader will think, so explain the "jobs" or the "positions" of Christ. He has three offices.

Scripture References: Jeremiah 10:10; John 18:37; Acts 3:22-23; Hebrews 4:15; Revelation 19:16.

Q. 65. What are they?
A. *The offices of a prophet, of a priest, and of a king.*

Explain what "prophet" and "priest" mean before going into *how* He fills each office. A prophet is one who can foretell the future and can tell you the will of God, because God talks directly to him. Christ is the only one who knows the plan God has willed for your life. Christ is also our priest, because a priest is a person who can talk directly to God. Christ talks directly to God for us.

Scripture References: Jeremiah 10:10; John 18:37; Acts 3:22-23; Hebrews 4:15; Revelation 19:16.

Q. 66. How is Christ a prophet?
A. *Because He teaches us the will of God.*

Only the Lord knows what He has planned for that child so parents ought to point their children to Him for direction. Truly the Bible says there is wisdom in much counsel, and parents should give a child counsel. But our counsel is for one reason: to point them to Christ as a prophet, for He teaches us the will of God. We ask it every time we pray the Lord's prayer. He taught us to pray, "Thy will be done." We should teach our children to include in their prayers "if it is Thy will." We say it and they don't know what we're talking about. When we ask God "if it is Your will," what we're saying is, "if this is your plan for my life." "You've got my life planned — I don't know the plan, but You do, so do this tomorrow if it's Your will. I would like to have so and so if it's in Your plan for my life." Christ our High Priest is the only one who can teach us the will of God.

Scripture References: John 1:4; John 14:26; John 15:15.

Q. 67. How is Christ a priest?
A. *Because He died for our sins and pleads with God for us.*

These are two of the things the priest did. He took the sacrificial animal, and killed it and offered it for the people. Then he took some of the blood behind the curtain and sprinkled it on the mercy seat. That represented the appeasing of the wrath of God, satisfying God's divine justice for that person out there. Before the priest killed that animal, the sinner laid his hands on its head. All this is in Leviticus. They laid their hands on the animal's head, symbolizing putting their sins on the animal. Then the priest killed the animal and that shed blood represented atonement for all their sins. What does that teach us? It teaches us an innocent substitute could die for us — so Christ is our substitute. It teaches us that when they put a crown of thorns on His head, they were fulfilling what sinners had done all their lives — putting their sins on Christ — so that He could carry their sins to the cross and die for them. Thus His office as priest is two-fold. The priest offered the sacrifice for the sins of the people, and he also prayed for them, as typified by the altar of incense in front of the curtain. The priest would burn incense there, because that was symbolic of the prayers of the saints mingled with the prayers of the high priest for the people. Why? Because we know not how to pray as we ought. We don't know for what to pray, so our High Priest is praying for us. Christ takes our prayers and mixes His own with them and presents them perfect to God the Father.

Scripture References: Romans 8:26-27; Hebrews 4:14-16; Hebrews 9:28; Hebrews 10:1-12.

Q. 68. How is Christ a king?
A. *Because He rules over us and defends us.*

"Defends us" means (for the little ones) "takes care of us; fights our battles." And that's not a bad idea of which to remind your older children because they get the big idea early that "I have to defend myself." It's a tragedy that so many well-intentioned parents say, "I have taught my son to take care of himself. I don't want him to hit first, but I want him to defend himself." That's no more Christian doctrine than heathenism. Christ said, "Don't worry if somebody hits you, just turn the other cheek and let him hit the other side." Christ set the example. *He* let them walk over Him! Why can we do that? Because our Lord (and every time you think His name, it ought to be in terms of His Sovereignty, majesty, and all His attributes,) loves me, and I'm one of His children. I can rest assured that He's not going to let any more happen to me than He wants to happen to me for my spiritual growth. Things that happen to me are to purify the silver and burn out the impatience and all the things wrong and sinful in my life, and to make me a better Christian. When I think of the Lord saying, "Vengeance is mine, I will repay," I realize nothing can harm me, because the Lord said, "I will never leave you nor forsake you — I will repay anybody that does anything to my child."

It's better to teach a child Scriptural principles in the beginning than to teach error with intentions of correcting it when they're older. Not to fight back is more wonderful, isn't it, than to fight back? It is just like a God who can't lie. It's more wonderful when the catechism says that God can do "all things" to know it means "everything good." True doctrine makes the Lord bigger and more wonderful. We Christian parents shield our children from sound doctrine. It is largely our fault that they aren't any better Christians than they are. How is Christ a king? Because He rules over us and defends us.

Scripture References: Proverbs 20:22; Isaiah 33:22; Acts 18:10; I Corinthians 15:25; II Corinthians 12:9-10.

Q. 69. Why do you need Christ as a prophet?
A. *Because I am ignorant.*

The prophet is the one who tells you the will of God for your life. What does the word "ignorant" mean? It means "I don't know anything." I'm ignorant. I need Christ as my prophet. He knows the will of God for my life. Can you see the assurance, the peace and joy a little tiny child can have with some understanding of the fact that Christ is our prophet? He knows how many children I'm going to have; He knows what school I'm going to attend; He knows whether I'm going to live to be grown or not; He knows what job I'll have (if I have a job). He knows whether I'll stay whole in body all my life or not. He knows because He planned it, and all I have to do is go to Him for guidance. I'm ignorant, but He can tell me what He wants of my life.

Scripture References: Psalm 73:22-24; John 20:31; II Peter 1:21.

Q. 70. Why do you need Christ as a priest?
A. *Because I am guilty.*

Underscore "guilty" because that means "I did it — I'm the one who is at fault." I know a little boy who has never yet ever been guilty. He can always explain why he did what he did, and why *he* was right. Everybody else was wrong. You're never going to need a Saviour until you are wrong, and that's true. A perfect person needs no saviour. I'm guilty.

Now review Questions 34 and 35 and 42 — all of these refer to the original part of the plan of salvation. We're all sinners, we've broken the covenant, we're condemned by it. The preacher still preaches to us adults that we're sinners and we still have to be reminded, so you're not going to overwork this doctrine.

Scripture References: Romans 3:23; Romans 12:10; James 2:10.

Q. 71. Why do you need Christ as a king?
A. *Because I am weak and helpless.*

The children don't even know He is their king! They think we have a president, and England has a king. They haven't thought about Christ as our king. We've explained that Christ has these three offices, and some day He's coming to rule in His glory. Now His kingdom is not of this world, it's a spiritual kingdom. He will rule in your heart if you allow Him to do so. To accept Him as your king is to accept Him as your employer, and to live by His rules, and to do things His way. I've worked for someone else. If any one of you has worked for someone else you know how much what you have to say matters, for who is the final authority? The boss! Until Christ is the final authority in your life He's not your king, because He's not ruling over you. We don't need Him as our king until we recognize that we're weak and helpless. What about big eighth-grade boys? They don't think they're helpless, and I'm not sure fourth-grade boys think they're helpless either. They can kick a football, they can fight. So we have a problem getting across to them that they are weak and helpless. The only way we can see ourselves is to look at God. When we look at Him, we hear Him saying, "I'm running this whole thing; no king gets on a throne unless I put him there, I will it." Nothing happens other than what God plans. Therefore I'm completely helpless. I *think* I can do things. I think I can drive the car. I think I can get back home. I think I can follow the directions. But you know, and every child knows, if he thinks about it, that I can't get home unless the Lord means for me to do so. Everything could happen to keep me from getting home if the Lord didn't mean for me to get there. I cannot overrule His will for my life. I am weak and helpless and this is an important thing for children to learn.

What offices has Christ? Christ has three offices. What are they? The offices of a prophet, of a priest, and of a king. Be sure the children know what a prophet is. He told the future, and the will of God for the people. We have examples of that. David wanted to build the temple, and Nathan the prophet told him to go ahead and build it. Then Nathan learned that God didn't mean for David to build it, but Solomon; so the prophet was to tell the will of God. Sometimes the kings would go to the prophets and ask, "Shall we go into this battle or not?" Sometimes the prophet would say, "Yes, the Lord wants you to go to battle." Other times he would say, "No, because He will not be with you."

Then review Question 69 with Question 66. I *didn't* say 66 with 69, because I would ask, "Why do you need Christ as a prophet?" Until they realize they *need* Christ as a prophet, "How Christ is a prophet?" doesn't mean much to them. The reason I need Christ as a prophet is that I am ignorant, and ignorant means I don't know what today is going to bring. I don't know what He wants of me tomorrow, and that is why I go to Christ in prayer and ask that His will be done, and ask that He teach me. Question 66 tells how Christ is a prophet ("because He teaches us the will of God") and until they realize that they need Christ as a prophet, you see, Question 66 doesn't have much meaning.

I would then review 70 with 67. "Why do you need Christ as a priest?" "Because I am guilty." Review Questions 34, 35, and 42, which state that everybody is a sinner. We have all fallen into sin through Adam's original sin, and you have references in Romans 3 that all have sinned. "Guilty" means that I am wrong, I have sinned, I have done wrong. Then Question 67 asks you, "How is Christ a priest?" "Because He died for our sins and pleads with God for us." If you really can see yourself as a sinner, as guilty, as doing wrong, then you know you deserve the wrath and curse of God. The high priest was the one who sprinkled the blood of the sacrificial animal on God's altar as atonement for sins, and he was also the one who prayed for the people.

This is the way Christ became our high priest: He died for our sins, He's the perfect sacrifice. And now He is sitting at the right hand of God the Father, interceding for us. "Pleads" means that He asks earnestly and boldly, He talks to God constantly for me. No matter what I do, Christ pleads His blood for my forgiveness. What I mean by "no matter" is that I cannot do anything that will undo my salvation. *You* can't undo your salvation, because *you* didn't do anything to get it! God gave it to you, and He says it's yours to keep. You could commit murder, or any sin, but you cannot undo your salvation. That's what I mean by "no matter".

It's hard to teach the **ABSOLUTENESS** of your assurance of salvation without seeming to contradict the doctrine of the perseverance of the saints. We have already talked a good bit about the good works and sanctification being fruit or results or products of our salvation. It is very important that, having emphasized the absolute trustworthiness of our High Priest in interceding for us at all times, we also emphasize the teaching that we are to remain in obedience to God's word; that we are to work out our own salvation with fear and trembling; that he who perseveres to the end is saved. This doctrine is hard for adults, but I don't believe we can minimize one side of it in order to do justice to the other side. If we teach Scripture as accurately as we can, no matter how difficult the doctrine or seeming contradiction, we can and must trust the Holy Spirit to apply it to the lives and understanding of the children. My salvation is assured because of the covenant between God the Father and God the Son. In Job we learn that the devil accuses the saints before God. But Christ is seated at the Father's right hand, saying, "I died for her, I purchased her redemption with my blood." It's as though God sees me through red plastic; He sees me through the shed blood of Christ, which washes me white as snow. That's why we need a priest, and that's how Christ is our priest. That He died for me is only part of it; the other part is that He is constantly pleading for me.

Then review 71 with 68. Why do you need Christ as a king? "Because I am weak and helpless." You'll have trouble making the children think they are helpless and that they are weak. But we are completely helpless in God's hands. He can change any one of us right this minute. We could become afflicted with some terrible disease, or we could die right now, or we could lose our homes, and all of these things would be out of our hands. We're completely helpless. We're in God's hands, to do with as He wills.

Then look at Question 68: "How is Christ a king?" (If I'm in this helpless condition I *need* a king.) "Because He rules over us and defends us." The beautiful lesson is that God says, "Vengeance is mine, I will repay." We don't have to fight back, and these children ought to learn it! A Christian parent can tell his child to turn the other cheek, or to walk away. That's what the Bible teaches, and God says He'll fight your battles for you. He's not going to let any more happen to His child than He intends to use to His glory. He allowed some of His children to be burned at the stake, and tossed by bulls, and sawn in sunder, but it was to accomplish His glory. Look what the blood of the martyrs did for the Christians through the years — it strengthened our faith and our Christian courage! We are weak and helpless in ourselves, but God is everything we need, and He will take care of us and defend us, and that is very important.

Scripture References: Exodus 14:14; Romans 7:15; II Corinthians 12:10.

Q. 72. How many commandments did God give on Mount Sinai?
A. *Ten commandments.*

You know, the Catholics say ten, but they leave out the second commandment and divide the tenth one in two. They say, "Thou shalt not covet thy neighbor's wife," Number 9, and Number 10, "Thou shalt not covet anything that is thy neighbor's, etc."
Does the Bible ever say there were 10? Yes, in Deuteronomy 10:4. I would read Exodus 19 and 20 to them, not word for word, but until you get the picture, then tell it to them. It's a marvelous story of how Moses went into Mt. Sinai and God gave him the ten commandments and he came back and told the people, and it frightened them. God said, "Don't let any of them come near this mountain." Who wrote the ten commandments? They were written with the finger of God. God wrote the ten commandments and gave them to Moses. It's interesting to remember that He wrote it with His finger and the only other time that the finger of God is mentioned, I believe, is when He is writing again. When the people accused the woman taken in adultery, Christ, who was also God, reached down and wrote in the sand. The same God who wrote the commandments with His finger is now writing in the

sand, forgiving the woman from the penalty of the law.

To whom were the ten commandments written? The prologue to the ten commandments is: "I am the Lord thy God, who hath brought thee out of the land of Egypt, out of the house of bondage." The ten commandments were given to God's children *after* He had saved them. He had brought them out of Egypt. He had saved them from the bondage of sin; then He gave them rules governing how they were to live as His children. Christ said, "I didn't come to do away with those; I came to explain them to you and to show you what they really mean."

Scripture References: Exodus 19 & 20; Deuteronomy 10:4.

Q. 73. What are the ten commandments called?
A. *The Decalogue.*

They're called the Decalogue. "Deca" is Latin. It is the same root word for decimal, meaning ten. "Logue" is the same word used for a ship's log, or a catalog, or a monologue. It's a listing or a saying. A dialogue is the saying between two people. A monologue is the saying of one person. A catalog is a multiple listing. So the two words put together give us the ten listings or the ten sayings of Jehovah. Those under the sixth grade probably won't appreciate that explanation, but the sixth-graders up should find it helpful.

Scripture References: Exodus 31:18; Exodus 32:15-16; Exodus 34:1;

Q. 74. What do the first four commandments teach?
A. *Our duty to God.*

Scripture References: Deuteronomy 6:5; Mark 12:29-30.

Q. 75. What do the last six commandments teach?
A. *Our duty to our fellow men.*

Scripture References: Deuteronomy 6:5; Deuteronomy 10:1-4; Leviticus 19:18; Romans 13:9-10.

Q. 76. What is the sum of the ten commandments?
A. To love God with all my heart, and my neighbor as myself.

Questions 74, 75, and 76 go together. The first four commandments teach our duty to God. Explain the word duty. It's our responsibility, it's what we owe to God, it's what He expects of us, it is what is required. The last six commandments teach us our duty to our fellow men — that is, what we owe to our fellow men. Some say that Jehovah probably wrote the first four commandments on one tablet, and the last six on the second tablet. Then explain that the sum of the ten commandments is the total when they are all added together. Define sum for the children. The ten commandments, then, all add up to loving the Lord with all your heart, and your neighbor as yourself.

It's a very good idea to have the children look up all the references on this question. This sum of the ten commandments was given in Deuteronomy 6:5, and Christ quoted it in the New Testament in Matthew 20. Christ said to love your neighbor as yourself. Ephesians 5:29 tells you how much you love yourself. That is how completely you are to love your neighbor. We instinctively try to protect ourselves from all harm. This is the way we are to feel about our neighbor. We always put self first. This is to be the attitude toward our neighbor (Phil. 2:4). We are to be as concerned about our neighbor's welfare as we are about our own. We see, then, just how far short we fall in obedience to this sum total of the law.

Scripture References: Deuteronomy 6:5; Matthew 22:37-40; Mark 12:30-31; Romans 13:9-10; Ephesians 5:10; I Thessalonians 4:9.

Q. 77. Who is your neighbor?
A. All my fellow men are my neighbors.

The story of the Good Samaritan teaches us that everybody is our neighbor. Everybody is my brother in that God created all men from Adam, one blood, but they are not all the children of God.

Creation does not make us children of God. It takes regeneration, re-creation, rebirth, to make us children of God. But we are still to love all men as souls. This does not mean going around saying, "I love everybody, there's nobody that I hate." We do not really love everyone; we indifferently tolerate most of them. This love is to manifest itself in a concern for their spiritual and physical well-being. If I am criticized, I should be just as quick to defend the one who criticized as to defend myself. It's important not to minimize what it means to love our fellow men as ourselves. This is God's perfect requirement. Let us strive toward perfection, and inspire this in our students.

Scripture Reference: Luke 10:30-37.

Q. 78. Is God pleased with those who love and obey Him?
A. Yes; He says, "I love them that love me."

Scripture References: Proverbs 8:17; John 16:27; Romans 8:28.

Q. 79. Is God displeased with those who do not love and obey Him?
A. Yes; "God is angry with the wicked every day."

Questions 78 and 79 need expounding a little because we are likely to teach a works salvation if we aren't careful. "Is God pleased with those who love and obey Him?" Yes, He says in Proverbs 8:17, "I love them that love me." Is God displeased with those who don't love Him and don't obey Him? Yes, Psalm 7:11 says, "God is angry with the wicked every day." Now angry is a good word, but we seem to have substituted "mad," and many of the little children may not even know what the word "angry" means. So explain that angry means mad or furious or whatever word they know. The wicked are the unregenerate. They are the ones who are not saved. They are not God's children. If we aren't careful, these two questions give a little child the idea that if I'm good God loves me, and if I'm bad He hates me, so that you can fall in and out of grace. We've already explained that we are saved as a free gift from God and there's nothing we can do to earn it. He keeps us; He doesn't let us fall out of His hand; nothing can take us out of His hands. So what do these words mean? It hurts God, grieves the Holy Spirit when the Christian disobeys God, but Question 79 is not talking about the Christian. Question 79 is talking about the person who is *not* one of God's children.

Question 78 says, "I love them that love me." A child knows that he doesn't love God as he should. In fact, to be honest, we don't either. God is something I can't see, but He has said we love Him because He first loved us. One of the things for which we pray is that we will love Him more. We sing, "More love to Thee, O Christ, More love to Thee." The Christian should constantly desire to love God more, to appreciate what He's done for us. The child who has come to Christ loves Him, and God loves that child. We don't love Him as we should, but this is not a fluctuating thing in your life (today I love Him, and I was good and He loved me, and tomorrow I do something bad and He gets mad at me). That's not it — and they're likely to get that picture if you don't explain that the wicked are the unregenerate.

Scripture Reference: Psalm 7:11.

Q. 80. Which is the first commandment?
A. *The first commandment is, "Thou shalt have no other gods before me."*

We could spend a whole day on this because "god" has to be explained. A "god" is the object of worship. With one child it is athletics, and he will have to be honest and admit that he likes athletics better than God. With another it is clothes. Christ had one garment, and He preached over and over, "Take no thought of what you are going to wear; the Lord is going to provide clothes." Almost all of us have clothes as a god, and we teach it to our children. It has become an honor to be the best dressed at school.

Can you imagine Christ getting that honor? We are guilty of teaching the worship of false gods to our children.

There are many gods. With another person good grades may be such a god, and he doesn't have time to read his Bible for studying. I've had college students tell me, "I know I don't get to Sunday School like I should, I know I don't have devotionals like I should, but I'm taking a heavy course and I've got to pass it." You see, there are numbers of things that come ahead of God, and the first commandment is, "Thou shalt have *no* other gods before Me." Thou shalt love the Lord with your whole mind; when you study, you study for God's glory. When you dress, you dress for God's glory, not because of what fashion requires, etc. This needs to be brought home to children, and remember this: you can hit a lot more forcefully with children the smaller they are, because as they begin to get older, parents and teachers and the world begin to cut down the ten commandments, so that when we teach they no longer hear us with the faith of a little child.

Scripture References: Exodus 20:3; Deuteronomy 5:7.

Q. 81, What does the first commandment teach us?
A. *To worship God alone.*

"Worship" means to put Him first, to adore Him, to praise Him. What a tragedy that even our secular music has become almost blasphemous. We sing, "I adore you!" and "adore" means "worship." You see, even a sweetheart puts a sweetheart ahead of God. We say, "This is heavenly," and it isn't. That is saying that this is so perfect in my eyes that it is just divine! Only God can be called those things. So when it says worship God alone it is striking down all our other gods.

Scripture References: Exodus 34:14; Psalm 29:2; Matthew 4:10; Matthew 6:33.

Q. 82. Which is the second commandment?

A. *The second commandment is, "Thou shalt not make unto thee any graven image, or any likeness of anything that is in heaven above, or that is in the earth beneath, or that is in the water under the earth: thou shalt not bow down thyself to them, nor serve them: for I the Lord thy God am a jealous God, visiting the iniquity of the fathers upon the children unto the third and fourth generation of them that hate me; and showing mercy unto thousands of them that love me, and keep my commandments."*

Underscore "graven." You will have to explain that a graven image is hand-made. Underscore "jealous" because God is jealous. It's all right for Him to be, but it's wrong for us to be jealous. It means that God does not want other people or things loved as much as He is loved. He must be first. It is wrong for me to be jealous, because for me to be jealous is for me to want to be first in someone's love. That is to be self-centered and love self. If I want you to love me more than you love anyone or anything else it's because I think of myself more highly than I ought to think. To rejoice with those who rejoice sometimes means to be genuinely happy when others receive a blessing you wanted very much for yourself. It's much more natural to be jealous of those people. This attitude is wrong for the Christian.

But because God is God, He has the absolute right to more love and honor than all else in our lives. He has a right to it because He is absolutely holy and pure and good, and absolute holiness and goodness *should* be loved above all else. His jealousy emanates from His absolute holiness.

This is an exceptionally hard lesson for the children, since it seems contradictory for God to be allowed to be jealous when this attitude is sinful in us. Do not hasten over it until you are fairly certain your pupils understand the difference, which is based on the holiness of God and the sinfulness of man. And remember that children find it very difficult to understand or accept their own sinfulness.

"Iniquity" means the wrong things you do, or the sins. Explain "generations." We have talked about that, when Adam represented all his posterity. Remind them again that generations cover those that come many years after. That doesn't mean that the grandchild of an unsaved person will never be saved. But the third and fourth generations will suffer when someone in that family turns his back on God. My grandparents sinned, but I'm not suffering for their sins, because they *loved* Him. "Unto the third and fourth generation of them that *hate* me, and showing mercy unto thousands of them that love me and keep my commandments..." Keeping His commandments is a result of loving Him. We don't get mercy because we keep the commandments; we keep the commandments because we love Him, and we love Him because we have already obtained mercy.

Scripture References: Exodus 20:4-6; Exodus 34:14; Deuteronomy 5:8-10.

Q. 83. What does the second commandment teach us?
A. *To worship God in a proper manner, and to avoid idolatry.*

John 4:24 is the classic example of worshipping God in a proper manner. Christ told the woman at the well in Samaria, "God is a spirit and they that worship Him must worship Him in Spirit and in truth." While it is true that to worship God in a proper manner means to worship with a pure heart, it is also true that a child cannot worship God in spirit and in truth unless he is a Christian. However, since this question deals with the manner, or method of worship, explain the importance of quiet reverent behavior in the Lord's house, and in places of prayer or instruction. Tell them, with great awe, the story of Isaiah in the presence of God in Isaiah 6, and how he fell on his face in reverence! Tell them how the apostles reacted when Christ stilled the storm at sea. Tell them the story of Christ's cleansing the temple and contrasting the purpose of the temple with their sinful use of it.

I believe many times children get a wrong concept of the holiness of God and the awesomeness of being in the presence of God from teachers who don't stress enough the importance of solemnity and reverence in worship. When a child is giggling or inattentive or in any way disrespectful during any part of the worship service, do you calmly and sweetly merely put your hand on his shoulder as a reminder to him to quit playing with Johnny in the seat next to him? Or is your attitude and approach at such times more in keeping with John 2:15-16?

Then of course, we must teach them to avoid the use of any statues or statuettes in worship. They should also be taught not to have any pictures of Christ, or worship centers as a stimulus to worship.

Scripture References: Exodus 34:14; Deuteronomy 4:15-19; I John 5:21.

Q. 84. Which is the third commandment?
A. The third commandment is, "Thou shalt not take the name of the Lord thy God in vain; for the Lord will not hold him guiltless that taketh His name in vain."

"Vain" means promiscuously, or lightly, or in fun. We are not to use God's name in any way except in perfect and complete reverence. For the Lord will not hold that person guiltless — "guiltless" means innocent. Anyone who has the habit of saying, "Oh, Lord," is guilty of sin before God. God will refuse to say that person is innocent and doesn't realize he is sinning, or doesn't know any better! One of the most important and reverent things in God's eyes is His own holy name. Read Ezekiel 36, beginning with the twentieth verse and see how God feels about His name. He says there, "You Israelites, which are my children — you Christians — turned against me. You didn't obey me, or honor me or love me, etc. These are your sins; nevertheless I will save you *for my great name's sake!*" And in other places He says, "You have desecrated my name, but I will bring you back for my holy name's sake." God places His name high and it is to be respected and revered by us. We pray that we'll keep this commandment every time we pray the Lord's Prayer. When the disciples asked Christ how to pray, He told them to call upon their Father in Heaven, and then He taught Christians to ask, "Lord, help me to remember to keep your name holy." "Hallowed be Thy name." "Hallowed" means sacred, holy, lifted-up, reverenced, set apart for God's service — sanctified.

Scripture References: Exodus 20:7; Leviticus 19:12; Deuteronomy 5:11; Isaiah 6:3; Matthew 6:9.

Q. 85. What does the third commandment teach us?
A. To reverence God's name, word and works.

Use the Shorter Catechism for help in explaining these answers. Go to Questions 54 and 55 of the Shorter Catechism, because it goes into these answers more fully so that you can better understand the doctrinal content and translate it into the child's language for him to understand. "God is a spirit, infinite, eternal and unchangeable in His being, wisdom, power, holiness, justice, goodness and truth." Any attribute of God is holy and to be reverenced as being fulfilled and complete only in God. Therefore, any time you use an attribute of God in swearing, or lightly in slang language, you are desecrating the name of God. My father wouldn't let me use slang, but even when I said, "My goodness," which was as strong language as I was allowed to use, I was calling upon one of God's attributes to testify to my sincereity, and so I was using God's name irreverently. Nothing is good except God. So when I say, "Good gracious," I am calling on the attributes of God to strengthen my language. We understand that all of our slang got started by the desire to call upon the name of God to witness to our statements, but not actually to say His name. So "Golly" or "Gosh" began to take the place of actually saying God. All of these were a way to get around saying "God" and thus swearing by the name of God. "Holy Cow," "Holy Smoke," "Holy Mackerel" — all are considered acceptable slang by men, but do you see how we are blaspheming the attributes of God by using these words lightly which describe God and God alone?
So we come to the question, "Well, what are we allowed to say?"

The Bible answers this simply enough! "Let your yea be yea and your nay be nay." Be the kind of person that tells the truth, so that when you say something you don't have to say, "Gosh yes!" You simply have to say, "Yes" — and from **YOU** that's sufficient! And **THAT'S** what the Bible requires of us. This is just another teaching that shows us how far afield of the commandments we've strayed. The fact that we don't live up to this command doesn't change the commandment. The law points its finger at our imperfections, not at the imperfections of the law.

Scripture References: Ezekiel 36:20-23; Matthew 5:33-37; James 5:12
Shorter Catechism References: Questions 54 and 55

Q. 86. Which is the fourth commandment?
A. *The fourth commandment is, "Remember the Sabbath day, to keep it holy. Six days shalt thou labor, and do all thy work: but the seventh day is the sabbath of the Lord thy God: in it thou shalt not do any work, thou, nor thy son, nor thy daughter, thy man-servant, nor thy maidservant, nor thy cattle, nor thy stranger that is within thy gates: for in six days the Lord made heaven and earth, the sea, and all that in them is, and rested the seventh day: wherefore the Lord blessed the sabbath day, and hallowed it."*

What is "holy"? Dedicated to God! Not only must His **NAME** be hallowed but His **DAY** must be hallowed. "Hallowed" means sacred, held high in reverence — a special day, different from every other day. There are frequent references in the Old Testament where Jehovah said, "You have not kept my commandments nor my Sabbaths." He put a special emphasis on the Sabbath, although it is included in the commandments. That's how important this is!

I'd like to give this word of personal testimony: I was raised in a church that taught that to keep this commandment only meant abstaining from anything commercial on Sunday. So not to buy gas, or not to pay to go swimming, or to a ball game or picture show made me a good girl. Frequently my husband and I would take the children and a picnic lunch on Sunday afternoon and spend the afternoon fishing. I felt so pious and good for spending the Sabbath in a way pleasing to God! Then when we discovered Isaiah 58:13-14, we learned that the Lord meant for us to abstain from all worldly pleasures, and to devote the entire day to praising and worshipping and honoring Him!

My daughters baby-sit. That's the way they earn their spending money. So when anyone calls them to baby-sit on Sunday, they can't do it, because they can't work on Sunday. However, when there is an emergency they do baby-sit, but they do not take money for it because Christ teaches us that it is right to do good to our fellow man on the Sabbath. When it is an act of service or help to our fellow man, it is good, but we are not to make it an act of work by accepting money for it. I believe this principle applies to every person working on Sunday. Our Lord approves acts of necessity and mercy; but any act, no matter how merciful it may be, is not an act of pure mercy when it is included on the payroll.

This principle might resolve our Sunday laws, if the Christians were obedient! There'd be many more stores closed on Sunday if everyone lived by this principle. We beat this commandment to pieces, but we don't change it! The commandment stands, as is, and God says to us, "Be ye perfect." These are the guidelines God gave to Christians. They're much higher than we can ever attain, but He doesn't smile and say, "I understand," when we break them. He says to strive toward perfection, and **CONFESS YOUR SINS** when you break them!

Now I have had to, and you may have to, teach this commandment to children whose parents keep their business open on Sunday. So let me remind you again of the Scripture in Ephesians 4 with which we started the course. We are to speak the truth in love, for the edifying of the saints. We are not to compromise with truth for fear of hurting feelings; we are to teach the Bible, the whole truth. But we are to do it in love, that we may all grow into perfection in Christ. God promises that where one plants the seed and another waters, God will bring forth the fruit.

Scripture References: Exodus 20:8-11; Deuteronomy 5:12-15.

Q. 87. What does the fourth commandment teach us?
A. To keep the Sabbath holy.

This means to keep it holy, hallowed, and sanctified. Deuteronomy tells us that God sanctified that day. The Bible goes into great detail to say that He sanctified that day. The vessels in the temple were sanctified, the priests were sanctified, and the word means set apart for God's service. Every Christian is sanctified by God. Sanctification is the work of God and it takes our lifetime as we yield more of our lives to Him and His service. The Sabbath day is to be kept holy, completely set apart for worship of God, and doing deeds of necessity and mercy.

Scripture References: Leviticus 19:30; Leviticus 23:3; Isaiah 58:13-14.
Shorter Catechism References: Questions 58, 60, 61 and 62.

Q. 88. What day of the week is the Christian Sabbath?
A. The first day of the week, called the Lord's day.

We have the Seventh Day Adventists and the Jews who say that the Sabbath is still the seventh day, because nowhere in the New Testament does it say, "Now it is no longer the seventh day, it is the first." We find in the history of the early church that it was changed to the first day of the week because Christ rose on the first day of the week. In Acts the apostles gathered together on the first day of the week; apparently the worship had been transferred from the seventh to the first. In I Corinthians, when Paul was telling the Christians how to conduct their worship, he said to gather the tithes on the first day of the week. So the offering became a part of the church service on the first day of the week. God required the first of everything. You see, it is not meant for the Christians just to be idle at the *end* of the week. No, you *start your week with God* on the first day of the week. I have to confess that for me the week ends on Saturday and Sunday and everything that I am going to begin, like a diet or anything of that kind, I start on Monday.

Therefore, I am still in a sense making Monday the first day of my week.

This is an example. My little sister, while in college, told our pastor that she was having such a hard time not studying on Sunday. She was carrying such a heavy course load and she was an honor student, which carried a lot of extra requirements. She tried so hard to get through by Saturday night, but she couldn't seem to do it. "I want to honor the Lord, and I want to give Him Sunday," she said, "but what do you do in a case like that? Do you just make bad grades?" He said, "Sandra, I think what you are doing is putting Sunday at the end of your week. You are trying to finish up your week with Sunday. Why don't you *start* your week with Sunday?" He said this one fall night at our house. That June when she graduated she said, "I want to give a testimony to the crowd: God told me to put Sunday first and I did. I started putting Sunday first. I would not open a book on Sunday, and what the Lord did for me was to increase my power of retention so that I studied a third as much as previously. I would retain what I studied, and I did not have to go back and dig. What I read stayed with me. This was the blessing that followed because I had obeyed His Word." So this is the first day of the week, although I have not learned to put it first in my week as I should. We need to teach it that way and strive to live up to this law as we teach it.

Scripture References: Acts 20:7; I Corinthians 16:2.

Q. 89. Why is it called the Lord's day?
A. *Because on that day Christ rose from the dead.*

I have noticed that many are calling Sunday "The Lord's Day." Instead of saying "Sunday," they say "next Lord's Day". It is a good way of reminding the Christian that this is a sanctified, hallowed, holy day set apart for God.

Scripture Reference: John 20:1,19.

Q. 90. How should the Sabbath be spent?
A. *In prayer and praise, in hearing and reading God's Word, and in doing good to our fellow men.*

Give examples in every one of those fields; also included here is resting the body.

He said, "Six days shalt thou labor." He took away the privilege of playing. If you look up Scripture on play, you will find that all are used in a derogatory sense. A Christian who plays may be an idle Christian and may be wasting his time. This is strong doctrine, and the more we grow spiritually, the more we understand this, for we are ever striving to be perfect as God would have us be. Prayer and praise would include Sunday night service, and it would exclude my using the Sabbath for my pleasure. I have finally gotten Sunday worked out so that I am fairly satisfied with it. Rather I can look over what I have done and be pleased at the progress I have made, but I can't look forward and be satisfied. I can, on Sunday afternoon, just sit down and thoroughly enjoy resting and relaxing. Nothing goes on at our house on Sunday afternoon. The "maid and the cattle" means for us the washing machine. I used to think that I could run a washing, for this is no work. But the Bible says don't operate anything that works for you. This is the afternoon that I get my Sunday School lesson, catechism and Bible study. I always have more Bible study than I can do. I look forward to doing some of it on Sunday afternoons.

We are learning from fellow Christians how to make Sunday what it should be. One person said his pastor does not listen to secular music on Sunday. My first reaction was, "How fanatical can you get!" But then our daughter wanted us to try it. We have some beautiful religious music and these records kept us conscious that this is Sunday, the Lord's Day. One Sunday night one of the college boys came in and sat down at the piano and started playing "Yellow Bird," and I thought our daughter was going to hit him! I had to remind her that where we had grown just a little bit and the Lord had blessed us with a little bit of what Sunday can mean to us, we don't judge what someone else does. Dr. Gutzke said that he taught his children not to buy anything on Sunday. (Do you know how many people will not buy their gas on Sunday?) He didn't buy anything on Sunday. One Sunday he took his children to town and they saw people buying ice cream cones and they said, "Bad people, bad people." He had to tell them that those people weren't bad, but *we* are different. Sunday has really been a blessing in our home. We have fallen so far short. As we tried to work out what to do with the children on Sunday afternoons, we began to buy Bible games and quizzes to use as a family. We are far beneath what we should be, but if we read the Bible, take what it says, and don't try to water it down, we will grow spiritually. Believe what it says, and He really blesses you, just like He says in Isaiah.

Scripture References: Isaiah 58:13; Matthew 12:12; Luke 4:16.

Review. By way of review let me ask you this: Who wrote the ten commandments? *God* wrote the ten commandments. To whom did He write them? To His own people. They are written to the Christians today. Why did He write them? Why did He give the commandments to His children? His law is perfect, and He gave us His commandments to show us what is required of man and what God expects. He says, "Be ye perfect as I am perfect," and this is your standard. Galatians 5:24 tells us what the law is. The law is a schoolmaster, to bring us to Christ that we may be justified by faith. Any time the commandments are taught and stressed as they should be, we will step on everybody's toes, for none of us keeps them perfectly. They are truant officers for Christ. We can stray away, and when we find that God does not want us to do something on Sunday, then the commandments serve as a truant officer to bring us back to Christ. Romans 10:4 tells us that Christ is the end of the law. Matthew 5:17 says Christ came not to destroy the law, but to fulfill it. Does this mean we are freed from the law? No, we are freed from the *curse* of the law. That is clarified in John 1:17 and Acts 13:39 and Galatians 3:13. The law has a finger to point at your sins, but it has no hand to help you. All the law does is condemn you. Grace reaches out with a helping hand and saves you. The law could never save you for you could never live up to it. We are never freed from *obedience* to it, but we are freed from obedience to it as a means of salvation. So the attitude of your heart when you live by it makes your obedience wrong or right. The Christian comes to love the law, the very thing that convicts him as a sinner. The Christian loves the law because it makes God's holiness so vivid. You can go right back to catechism question number 3, for you see, even the law glorifies God. The bigger our God is, the more wonderful He is to us and the more we love Him. When we really see ourselves as sinners, He becomes more wonderful to us. So we are freed from the curse of the law. It cannot condemn us to eternal death. We are saved through grace. But obedience is required as an act of love for the wonderful salvation that He has given us. It is His standard, and if I want to grow spiritually these are the steps by which I grow. I try to obey these commandments because I want to grow to please God. We are never excused from these reasons. Psalm 119 is the longest chapter in the Bible. It has 150 or more verses and all of these verses except two speak to us about the law of God. The quotation in verse 2 of Psalm 1 is, "But his delight is in the law of the Lord, and in his law doth he meditate day and night." Verse 105 of Psalm 119 says, "It is a lamp unto my feet and a light unto my path." All of these say that the law of God is correcting us. Romans 7:15-16 and I Timothy 1:8 tell us if we differ with the Ten Commandments it is not that the law is imperfect, but that we have fallen short. The first four commands tell us the duty of man to God. There is no other God before God. The last six tell us our duty to our fellow man.

Q. 91. Which is the fifth commandment?
A. *The fifth commandment is, "Honor thy father and thy mother: that thy days may be long upon the land which the Lord thy God giveth thee."*

This commandment is the only one with a promise. The only

word which should have to be explained is "honor." It means to learn to obey. Honor means to bring honor to the name of the family. It may be that my daddy or my mother may be the kind of person that does not deserve honor. They are not honorable people. My mother may be the kind of person that is everything of which I am ashamed. The child can bring honor to the name of the family by the way he behaves and by his conduct. He can rise in sanctification and in spiritual growth to the place that he is in favor with God and man, and he can bring honor to the family name. Thus he brings honor to the name even though his parents may not be honorable people. The child will bring honor to the parents in this way, even though they may not deserve honor. Thus the child is not excused from honoring his parents. The children are taught to obey their parents. When they reach the age of maturity and are no longer under the roof of their parents and no longer dependent upon their family and are the head of a family of their own, yet they are always under the rule of honor. As long as we live, and no matter how childish any of our parents get in old age, we are never excused from honoring them. The Bible tells us that we are responsible for our parents even when we get out from under their authority; we are still held accountable for taking care of them and providing for their needs. The Bible pronounces strong condemnation on the person who does not take care of the widows and orphans in his own family. Christ condemned the corban gifts which were given to keep from giving to the parents. The scribes and pharisees pronounced all of their wealth corban in order to get out of taking care of their poor, aging parents, but in their hearts they were not giving it to the glory of Christ. When they used it to take care of their parents, they were using it for the glory of Christ. Of course, there is a promise that goes with this, "...that thy days may be long in the land which the Lord thy God giveth thee." Here is the problem. Some child that these children may know may die early in life and he/she has lived a clean life that is an honor to his/her parents, so we must teach them that all of God's promises are based upon His own will.

None of us is going to die until God is through with us here on this earth. This does not mean I honor my parents in order to live a long time. The general rule applies that God honors the life of the person who honors his parents the way the Lord would have him honor them. China is the oldest country in the world. Many nations have risen and fallen and China has remained. They are one of the few peoples that place a high honor on parents. The parents are always honored and given a high place as head of the house; and China has outlived many nations. It is an interesting comment.

Scripture References: Exodus 20:12; Deuteronomy 5:16.

Q. 92. What does the fifth commandment teach us?
A. *To love and obey our parents and teachers.*

By "our parents" is meant all adults in authority over the children. We as teachers must keep that child disciplined and under control while in Bible school, Sunday school, catechism class, or if playing at our homes. The Scripture says the child is under the law. A child learns obedience while a child. It is important that he learn to respect authority and obey the law, else he may be the very one to break the speed laws or run a traffic light when no one else is looking. We ourselves must be careful to set a good example, for the child must have respect for the law and for those in authority.

We, as adults, have a responsiblity to demand honor and respect when we are in command over them.

Scripture References: Exodus 21:15, 17; Ephesians 6:1-2.

Q. 93. Which is the sixth commandment?
A. *The sixth commandment is, "Thou shalt not kill."*

Some of the children will ask questions such as: "Does this mean not to kill bugs?" The Hebrew word used here means "murder."

(Notice that we are going much faster now, covering more material than we covered in one session in the beginning. Lay a solid foundation in the first questions, and just go back to those principles which were established earlier.)

Now the question of capital punishment may come up. This principle taught by God is that a man who takes the life of another shall by man have his life taken. When a person kills another he is attacking the image of God. We see in Romans 13 that capital punishment is still proper and scriptural, never having been abrogated (See Question 20 explanation.)

Scripture References: Exodus 20:13; Leviticus 24:17; Deuteronomy 5:17; Romans 13:9.

Q. 94. What does the sixth commandment teach us?
A. *To avoid angry passions.*

You should explain the words "avoid" and "angry" and "passions." "Passions" means emotions and feelings. "Angry" means hateful and mad. To "avoid" means to stay away from. We are to try not to have bad feelings toward others.

In Matthew 5:21ff Christ interprets this commandment for us, and follows that with directives as to the proper procedure at times when you've offended or been offended. You don't let the sun go down, nor do you go to the Lord's table until you have first been reconciled to your brother. You see how important it is not to let this matter separate you. First, go to your brother and be reconciled with him. A minister once began a sermon regarding a controversial issue by saying that his congregation did not have to agree with him, but that the Bible said they did have to love him. This is the crux of the sixth commandment, to replace anger with love.

It may surprise a child to realize he is breaking the sixth commandment when he fights with another child, or hits another child. Refer to the explanation of Question 68. The Lord told us to turn the other cheek in situations of this kind because He, our Father, will fight our battles for us, for vengeance belongs to Him alone. You may be teaching children whose parents have taught them to "defend themselves" by fighting back when struck. It may be possible to defend one's self without anger, but very likely, when a child hits back, it is simply because he is angry!

Also this commandment teaches us to take proper care of our bodies, as the temples of the Holy Spirit, since it is also wrong for us to do those things that tend to destroy our own bodies. I believe many Christians are destroying their own bodies today with junk foods, lack of proper exercise, and indulgence of negative emotions such as anxiety, anger, temper, covetousness, hate, frustration, worry, etc. This subject can be pursued at length if necessary to get the point across.

Scripture References: Genesis 9:5-6; Leviticus 19:17-18; Matthew 5:21-26; Matthew 26:52.

Q. 95. Which is the seventh commandment?
A. The seventh commandment is, "Thou shalt not commit adultery."

I had a third-grader ask me what one word in the seventh commandment meant and guess what that word was? It was "commit." It means to do, and when he found out what that word meant, that took care of the seventh commandment as far as he was concerned! He didn't know what the Lord had said not to do, but that did not disturb him. Dr. Gutzke said that when he first read this commandment he thought it was some old custom of the Canaanites, and it didn't concern him either! So it won't bother the children as much as it will the teacher who anticipates their questions. Of course there are some for whom you have to be ready. With the little ones you start with pure foods. Pure lemon juice is lemon juice and nothing else. Unadulterated foods means nothing whatsoever has been added.

Scripture References: Exodus 20:14; Deuteronomy 5:18; Matthew 15:19; Matthew 19:1-12,18; Mark 19:2-12; Luke 16:18; 18:20; Romans 12:9.

Q. 96. What does the seventh commandment teach us?
A. *To be pure in heart, language and conduct.*

It is commanded that we have no impurity in our heart, which must be explained as meaning our thoughts, our language, which is the way we think and the things we say, and our conduct, which is the way we act and the things we do.

You can start with the fact that this commandment teaches purity. Anything that is unadulterated is pure. It teaches that your mother and daddy are not to make love to anybody but each other. God created Adam from the ground, and made Eve from the body of Adam — and man and wife are one in the eyes of God and nothing can separate them. Much of the child's security lies in the love the parents manifest for each other. To adulterate that love is to desire or entertain thoughts of that marriage relationship with another other than the mate. But now the morals of America seem set against the institution of marriage, and children cannot escape hearing it from many sources. It is vitally important, therefore, that we show them in Scripture what the Lord's directives are.

A child can break this commandment by watching an R-rated movie, by reading a sex-oriented magazine, by listening to certain songs over the radio. Even the TV commercials are aimed at causing lust in our hearts.

Since first giving these lectures, the morality of America has degenerated so rapidly, and sex has become such a popular subject, I have had to alter my suggestions regarding the teaching of this commandment. I am still convinced that children who have been protected from the filth of TV and picture shows and the wrong books will **NOT** be ready for the marriage relationship to be explained to them until they are reaching puberty. But since many parents are not protecting them from the seductive voice of the radio advertisement, or the scantily clad seducer of the TV commercial, or the everyday advertisements in magazines and newspapers, the explanation may have to come sooner. I do warn parents and teachers, however, not to assume the child knows as much as you think he knows; do give him the benefit of a little naivety. A child can see a seductive scene on TV or movie, and think merely that that man and that lady want to kiss and hug and they aren't supposed to because they aren't married to each other, and yet the adult thinks the child knows what the scene is really trying to portray (the real intent of the situation). In teaching children today, however, we have the sad problem of having to teach children whose parents have not been proper guardians of what the child sees or hears. Parents have done their children a great wrong by not supervising very closely what programs they are hearing and watching, and what daily conversations they may be overhearing. There is far too much of this subject already being thrown at our children from all sources — even the pulpit! I believe with all my heart that it is the privilege and duty of Christian parents to teach sex to their own children.

Teach them that the Lord is the one who is preparing a husband or wife for them right now; that they break this commandment by trying to dress in a way so as to attract the other sex. They break this commandment in telling dirty jokes or laughing at dirty stories. They must learn to turn the TV off if it offends in this area. They must be willing to refuse to give a book report in school if it requires the reading of filth. I would suggest talking with them until you determine where they are in their knowledge, and then deal with them from there. Although you may be laughed at, teach them the sanctity of the physical touch. They flirt with danger who hold hands, put their arms around each other, and indulge in physical contact of this nature on the single side of marriage.

This commandment does not allow for divorce other than for unfaithfulness. You may have a child in your class who is from a divorced home. Be sure you teach that _all_ of us have broken this commandment one way or another. There is none guiltless.

Scripture References: Matthew 15:19; 19:1-12,18; Philippians 4:8.

Q. 97. Which is the eighth commandment?
A. _The eighth commandment is, "Thou shalt not steal."_

The children know what these words mean but they may not

understand all the implications. This commandment covers stealing information in school. Cheating is stealing something that does not belong to you. It includes picking up something on the street that someone else has lost. When a person has lost something he looks for it along the route he's been, and if you leave the object there the owner may come back and find it. Someone else may pick it up first if you don't, that's true! But you're responsible for YOU, NOT SOMEONE ELSE! This commandment includes stealing time — making someone wait for you, being late for appointments and dates. This commandment includes picking flowers in someone else's yard without permission; breaking or rendering unusable another person's property. Included in this commandment is the forbidding of taking cookies from Mother's cookie jar without permission. I don't think we realize how often a child is tempted to take something that belongs to another. They slip things much more often than adults are aware. This commandment (as all the others) needs to be taught with much prayer that the Holy Spirit will apply it to the hearts of children.

Scripture References: Exodus 20:15; Deuteronomy 5:19.

Q. 98. What does the eighth commandment teach us?
A. *To be honest and industrious.*

Explain "industrious" for it means to work for what you get. What is wrong with stealing? It is a sign of laziness. We are showing that we are not willing to work for what we get. We are taking from the other person his right to ownership. We are transgressing his freedom to do with his own as he wishes. The Scripture teaches us to work for what we get, and not to expect something free. This commandment also covers the sin of trying to get a merchant to lower his retail price so that we won't have to pay so much for the article, which is a way of our stealing part of his profit — hunting for something that is worth more to us than to the person selling it and than we are willing to pay. This commandment also includes borrowing and not returning. If we lend, we are to expect nothing in return. If we borrow something and never return it or repay it, or if we break it in any way, then we have stolen.

Ephesians 4:28 teaches us that it is not enough not to steal, or ask for things, but we are to provide our own needs, and then to be concerned that the other person's needs are met also. The fulfilling of this law is to love our fellowman as ourselves. If we do this we will be as concerned with helping them acquire what they want or need as we are meeting our own needs or desires.

Scripture References: Exodus 20:15; Leviticus 19:11,13; Deuteronomy 5:19; Romans 13:9; Ephesians 4:28.

Q. 99. Which is the ninth commandment?
A. *The ninth commandment is, "Thou shalt not bear false witness against thy neighbor."*

"Bear false witness" has to be explained. "Bear" means to carry from one person to another. If you tell something, you have borne it. "False" means incorrect or untrue. "Witness" is a testimony. You are not to tell something that is untrue about the other fellow. "Neighbor" of course was explained in Question 77. You can't tell incorrect statements about anybody, because all of your fellowmen are your neighbors. This commandment forbids our telling tales or repeating what's been told us about another person, even if we believe our information is true, though we have no proof.

Scripture References: Exodus 20:16; Deuteronomy 5:20; Romans 13:9; I Timothy 5:13.

Q. 100. What does the ninth commandment teach us?
A. *To tell the truth.*

I believe this commandment means for us not to lie, or gossip, or be a tale-bearer. We are not to misrepresent any product or item for sale, not to withhold information that is advantageous to the other person's interests, and not to distort the pure truth in any way. But suppose that the tale I heard on someone else is true, and happened exactly as reported. Am I allowed then to tell it, if it is truth? No! The Scriptures require me to go directly to the person, and admonish and reprove and correct and instruct, if a brother be overtaken in a fault. But I am warned often in Proverbs not to be a bearer of tales.

Paul said, "For I determined not to know anything among you, save Jesus Christ, and him crucified."

Scripture References: Leviticus 19:11; Proverbs 21:6; I Corinthians 2:2; Ephesians 4:25.

Q. 101. What is the tenth commandment?

A. The tenth commandment is, "Thou shalt not covet thy neighbor's house, thou shalt not covet thy neighbor's wife, nor his manservant, nor his maidservant, nor his ox, nor his ass, nor anything that is thy neighbor's."

Every child will tell us he does not want Johnny's possession, he just wants one like it! "He can keep his, I just wish I had one, too." Coveting is taught us twenty-four hours a day in advertisements. We are taught to long for or desire or want (this is what covet means) many things that we do not have. To covet is to wish to be placed in another income-bracket other than the one in which the Almighty God has placed us. I approach this question pretty much the same for all ages, for even grown people, often, do not fully grasp that wanting something because you saw someone else with it is a sin. The children must be told that if a friend has a faster bicycle than theirs, and they are jealous, this is coveting. If someone else lives in a prettier house than theirs, they may be covetous. If they are envious of the person with his own swimming pool, this is coveting. If they resent the lack of the freedom another child has, this is coveting. To want to play with the toy a sibling is playing with is coveting.

Scripture References: Exodus 20:17; Deuteronomy 5:21.

Q. 102. What does the tenth commandment teach us?
A. *To be content with our lot.*

How many adults have caused children to covet with the question, "What do you want for Christmas?" How many parents and grandparents have taught children to be discontent with their lot by giving them too much of this world's goods! Truly happy is the person who has learned to be content with his or her lot. It is one secret to being able to rejoice with those that rejoice. Secular sciences teach us that frustrations, resentments, unfulfilled desires, etc., can and do cause many of our most common illnesses. What an important opportunity to teach children that they are sinning as much as if they were murdering when they desire what they do not have! We must, after teaching them what the sins are, teach them to go to the Lord in constant confession of coveting, envy and jealousy, and to plead for grace to be content with their lot. It may help them for you to teach them that lust, greed, and covetousness are *never* satisfied. A person can *never* own so much that the old nature would be satisfied and never desire more, or a newer model or a larger or more expensive product. Just think of it! Covetousness can *never* be satisfied for very long. Please try to help the children see this! Use specific examples, according to their age level, and talk about it until they've gotten the point. Help them, instead of concentrating on coveting, to concentrate on using what they already have to the glory of God.

Scripture References: Proverbs 17:5; 24:17-19; Philippians 4:11-13.

Q. 103. Can any man keep the ten commandments perfectly?
A. *No mere man, since the fall of Adam, ever did or can keep the ten commandments perfectly.*

We have a tendency to teach children to "be good" and not to be "bad" as though this could be accomplished through sheer determination. If we have done a good job of teaching what the ten commandments actually require, the children should realize that no one can be as good as God wants him to be.

Your cross reference here will be Question 42. Don't forget that we keep going back so that the whole catechism will unfold to the children as a unified, connected system of doctrine. Why can I not be saved by the covenant of works? Because all have broken it and are condemned by it. We could also go back to 34, 35 and 36. When Adam sinned, he represented all his posterity; all of us are born in a state of sin and misery. This is original sin. All of us have broken the law and are condemned by it. Question 70: Why do you need Christ as a priest? Because I am guilty. Of what are you guilty? I am guilty of sin, guilty of having a sinful nature. For all of these reasons, no man since the fall of Adam has kept or can keep the ten commandments perfectly. Stop here and explain fall. Explain that the "fall of Adam" was the "sin of Adam." This is when he sinned and ate the forbidden fruit. This is the original sin. So no man, since Adam sinned, ever did or can keep the ten commandments perfectly. Then if you can't keep them, what good are they?

Scripture References: Deuteronomy 27:26; I Kings 8:46; Galatians 3:10; James 2:10.

Q. 104. Of what use are the ten commandments to us?
A. *They teach us our duty, and show our need of a Saviour.*

Every once in a while word your questions in everyday language, or the child's language. Try to trip them up, because what you really want to do is see if they are getting the sense of the question and the sense of the answer. So that is what the 104th question is asking you; what good are the ten commandments if you can't keep them? We learned that they teach us what God expects of us. They teach us the perfection of God. This is His perfect standard. Man can never reach it. We all have learned that we can't live those ten commandments. They show us our duty to

God and our duty is to live perfectly, for He said, "Be ye perfect as I am perfect." Our duty is to strive to live a perfect life. We are to strive to attain perfection. Our duty is two-fold, as explained in Questions 74 through 76. The first four commandments tell us our duty to God, and the last six tell us our duty to our fellowman. So the ten commandments teach us our duty to God and our duty to our fellowman. Immediately when we see the perfection of the ten commandments and the sinfulness of man, what else do we see? We see our need of a Saviour. There you have another opportunity to present the plan of salvation. **DON'T EVER LOSE SIGHT OF THE FACT THAT YOU ARE NOT ONLY TEACHING THE CATECHISM MEMORIZATION, BUT YOU ARE TEACHING TO SAVE SOULS AND LIVES FOR CHRIST**. We want those who know Christ to live as Christians. We don't want those children to live carnal lives, but to shine for Christ. That is why we are teaching. So give the plan of salvation in the 104th Question. We need Christ as our Saviour to save us from our imperfections. Because if you can't get to Heaven by living the law perfectly, what is the only other way you can get there? Somebody has to live that law perfectly for us, and has to pay the penalty for the fact that we didn't. Christ did this for us. God, who inspired the Bible, says you must believe it to go to Heaven. There you see how important this question is.

Scripture References: Deuteronomy 27:27; Romans 3:20; Galatians 5:24.

Q. 105. What is prayer?
A. *Prayer is asking God for things which he has promised to give.*

Here we get into the Lord's prayer. I recommend two books for your library. One is **With Christ in the School of Prayer** by Murray, and the other is **The Harmony of the Westminster Standards** by Green. The latter contains and compares the Confession of Faith, the Larger Catechism, and the Shorter Catechism. It gives all the doctrine of our church, and you should have it for the time when you get into the commandments and the Lord's Prayer. You should know what the Confession of Faith says about them for your own background. We should learn as much strong doctrine as we can, then give it to the children in their own language.

I used to have trouble with this definition of prayer. "Prayer is asking God for things which he has promised to give." This leaves out thanksgiving, praise, confession (except that He has promised to give forgiveness). I think that when you read your Scriptural background for this question you will see that Philippians 4 says, "With praise and thanksgiving let your requests be known unto God." So thanksgiving in the Bible may not be considered prayer. Praise may not be considered prayer. Our interpretation of prayer is that it has five parts — praise, thanksgiving, confession, petition, and intercession. All of these are prayer to us. For children I cannot find much fault with the catechism answer so you can sum it up with three words, the secret of the happy Christian life for the adult. Do you know what that is? **CLAIMING THE PROMISES.**

There is a fine little book called, **The Unfailing Promises** put out by the Board of Women's Work of the P.C.U.S. It has 365 promises in it, a promise for every day of the year. You can live a triumphant Christian life claiming the promises. God has promised strength in time of weakness. You may utterly fail in time of weakness, for He is not bound to give you the promises unless you claim them. I have heard Dr. Gutzke give the example of the blackberry patch. There was a vacant lot nearby which had beautiful blackberries, and the lady who owned the lot never picked them. He asked if she wanted the berries and she said he could have all the berries he wanted. He loaded pails and buckets and went into the lot to pick the berries and guess how many he got? Just as many as he picked. That is the way with the promises. They are perfect for us. They are ripe and ready to be picked. God does not automatically give me strength, but the day I find the promise in which He says, "My strength is made perfect in your weakness," then as I claim that promise, He gives me strength. I may have been doing things all these years in my own strength, but what a blessing when I find this truth given by God. So it would be good if we could teach a whole course to those children on the promises. Get them to find the promises that God has for our claiming in the Bible. Why do we (as children) not fight other children? Because God has promised to fight our battles, and that vengeance belongs to Him. Why do we pray, "Give us this day our daily bread"? Because of the promises in Psalm 23:1 and Philippians 4:19. What promise has God for me if I am afraid of the dark? Many! He will never leave us or forsake us. He keeps us in the palm of His hand and underneath are the everlasting arms. He has promised to teach us how to love the brethren. This is something with which the child has trouble. It is difficult for them to love the old pious women and men. There are many promises for these children and this is really a terrific answer.

Scripture References: John 15:7; Philippians 4:6; I John 3:22; 5:14-15.

Q. 106. In whose name should we pray?
A. *Only in the name of Christ.*

This is something really important for your children to grasp. "Only in the name of Christ." We refer to Question 67 in the catechism. How is Christ a priest? Because He died for our sins and pleads with God for us. Where is the first person of the Trinity? He is seated on the throne. Where is the second person of the Trinity? He is sitting on the right hand of God interceding for the sinners. Where is the third person of the Trinity? He is in our hearts and Romans says He is praying for us with groanings that cannot be uttered. Why? Because we know not how to pray as we should. We don't know how to pray. We don't know how to ask for the things that are good for us. We may ask for something that really would be terrible if it happened, but the Holy Spirit is within us praying for us. Christ, the second person of the Trinity, is seated at the right hand of God interceding for me. A study of the tabernacle in Exodus tells us that the incense which went up daily was a type of the prayers of the saints which were mingled with the prayers of Christ. Christ takes our prayers and makes them perfect by adding His own to them. Christ presents them to the Father. What is the Father doing with our prayers? Isaiah says that before we ever say it, the answer is on the way. So we see that we have all the persons of the Trinity working for the Christian in prayer life. We pray only in the name of Christ. What do we say at the end of a prayer just before we say "Amen"? "In Christ's name we pray," or "For Christ's sake." Now if we pray for Christ's sake, it means that we want our petition for Christ's sake, because He died for us. That will change our whole prayer life if we stop to think what we are saying.

For example, my mother lives alone and there will be times when I am so concerned for her that I will say, "Lord, please do this for my mother's sake. She is such a wonderful Christian." Then I stop and think that anything done for my mother will not be for her sake, but it will be for Christ's sake. She is one of God's children and because Christ died for her, she is adopted into the Kingdom of Heaven. He has promised provision, help, mercy and protection in time of need to His children; so any of those things He gives her which He has promised, will be given for Christ's sake.

There are certain things I have had on my prayer list about which I can say, "For Christ's sake," because I know that for which I am asking can be to the glory of God. God can grant it because Christ died for me. I have had to scratch some things off my list for I really don't want them for Christ's sake. I don't want them for God's glory. It is just lust of the flesh. I just desire it, and not for Christ's sake. I can't ask God to give me the things I want because I am His child unless my receiving those things is for His glory.

Scripture References: John 14:13-14; 15:16; 16:24.

Q. 107. What has Christ given us to teach us how to pray?
A. *The Lord's Prayer.*

Use this question as a springboard to tie in Old Testament and New Testament praying. In the Old Testament the person praying cried out to Jehovah God as Adonai, El-Shaddai, Jehovah, Elohim, etc., names meaning Almighty, Covenant God, Lord of Hosts, All-Sufficient, Creator God, etc. God had revealed Himself to His

people by all of these names and attributes. But they had never
known Him as *Father* before. Jesus called Him "Father" so much
of the time, saying He and the Father were one, He was sent by the
Father, etc. And He spent SO MUCH time in prayer. It was natural
that the disciples felt that His prayer life had a quality about it
theirs didn't have, and they wanted to know how to pray as **HE**
prayed. As far as I know, this is the first time they were told directly
that they could call God "Father..." Imagine their consternation at
this! They had brought lambs and animal offerings to the Temple
all their lives to atone for their sins, and the high priest had played a
large part in their spiritual lives. Now here was Jesus not only
telling them they were to address Jehovah as their Father, but also
as though they were all brothers, *our* Father. Imagine coming to
Jehovah God in such familiar terms! And then He taught them to
ask for such unusual things. The six petitions in the Lord's Prayer
cover just about everything for which we'd pray. For this reason I
don't believe the Lord meant for us to "recite" it so much that it
becomes "rote" to us, which tends to make it less meaningful than it
should be.

You'll notice that the first three petitions ask for things pertaining
to the glory of God (just as the first four commandments are
regarding our duty to God), and then the last three petitions ask for
things pertaining to our needs (just as the last six commandments
pertain to our duty to our fellowman). This, probably, was to serve
as sort of an "outline" for us to follow in our own praying. It would
be good to let the children pray some prayers that would follow
this outline but still be personalized. For instance, instead of saying
"forgive us our debts" one might write in one of his own sins with
which he is dealing, of which he is conscious, and over which he
desires victory, Instead of "lead us not into temptation" one might
write in a request that the Lord be very close to him in a certain test
at school and protect him from cheating. The Lord's Prayer would
likely become much more meaningful to the children if they spent
some class time personalizing it in this manner.

You might share with the older children the fact that this was not
the way Christ prayed, for He had no sins to confess. His prayer is
contained in John 17, and is called Christ's high-priestly prayer. I

believe what we call the Lord's Prayer should better be called the Christian's Prayer. You see, we have an example of the unregenerate's prayer in the publican who smote upon his breast and said, "God be merciful to me, a sinner." This is the prayer that must be prayed by a non-Christian, because *God* is the *judge*, a more impersonal name than Jehovah. The only time Christ called Him "God" was on the cross when He cried out, "Why hast thou forsaken me?" God, dealing with sin, had indeed turned His back on the sacrifice for our sins. That's why it's so precious to us that at the last Christ cried out, "It is finished!" The work He had come to do, the work of dying for our sins, was finished. And then, "**FATHER**, into thy hands I commend my spirit." The debt had been paid, the Father's back was turned no more!

As good background reading for this question, I recommend **NAMES OF GOD** by Nathan J. Stone. This will help you, the teacher, understand the wonder and thrill of being able to call Jehovah God our *Father*.

Scripture References: Matthew 6:9-13; Luke 11:2-4; I John 5:14.

Q. 108. Repeat the Lord's Prayer.
A. *"Our Father which art in Heaven, Hallowed be thy name. Thy kingdom come. Thy will be done in earth, as it is in Heaven. Give us this day our daily bread. And forgive us our debts, as we forgive our debtors. And lead us not into temptation, but deliver us from evil: For thine is the kingdom, and the power, and the glory forever. Amen."*

We will have to explain "hallowed," "debtors," "debts," "temptation," "deliver" and "glory." All of these words are later taken up in the questions on the petitions.

Scripture References: Matthew 6:9-13; Luke 11:2-4.

Q. 109. How many petitions are there in the Lord's Prayer?
A. *Six.*

"Petitions" means askings. When we draw up a petition it is something for which we are asking; something that we want. Remember that those petitions cover those things we want. They are things that God has promised to give us.

Q. 110. What is the first petition?
A. *"Hallowed be thy name."*

The first thing we ask God for that He has promised to give is a reverence for His holy name. That is, that His name be kept holy. "Hallowed" means to keep it holy and reverent, to stand in awe of it, to keep it set apart for worship, praise, salvation and petition, and for things that are dedicated to God. It means not to use His name loosely. We covered this in the third commandment, how to pray that His name will be kept hallowed.

Scripture References: Deuteronomy 5:11; Ezekiel 20:7; 39:7,25; Matthew 6:9; Luke 11:2.
Cf. Questions: 3, 84-85.

Q. 111. What do we pray for in the first petition?
A. *That God's name may be honored by us and all men.*

In Question 111ǀ we take students back to Questions 84 and 85. What does the third commandment teach us? To reverence God's name, word and work.

Scripture References: Psalm 67:3; Psalm 145; Romans 11:36; IIThessalonians 3:1.
Cf. Questions: 84-85.

Q. 112. What is the second petition?
A. *"Thy kingdom come."*

This petition refers to the second coming. He has promised it and we are to ask for it. The next-to-last verse in the Bible is "Even so, Lord Jesus, quickly come." The Prince has promised to come, and the Bible closes with, "Hurry up and come." That is the prayer of the Christian. He who testifieth these things says, "Surely I come quickly. Amen." "Even so come, Lord Jesus." This is the hope of the Christian, and we pray that Christ will come soon. Please present the second coming of Christ with much enthusiasm and joy! Strive to get the children to anticipate Christ's coming with genuine pleasure. Tell them that when the Lord allowed John a glimpse into Heaven He told him not to write what he saw. We are to anticipate by faith and not by sight. It is so wonderful, far better than anything on this earth! Have the students name some of the joys of Heaven. *Child Evangelism* material is helpful in this. There are no tears, always joy, no medicine, because no sickness; no afternoon naps or early bedtime, because no night. No tears means no disappointments, no cuts or bruises or hurts, no hurt feelings.

Some child may ask regarding the presence of candy, ice cream, etc. in Heaven. Sometimes it is difficult to communicate the idea of perfection in Heaven to children whose ideas of causes of joy aren't up to the standards of our Lord. Remind them that it's not the presence of things as we know them on earth that brings complete happiness in Heaven, but the presence of a Person. With all the men who were present when Christ preached, He was the one to whom children were drawn. Isn't it exciting! Jesus is so wonderful that when God let John see into His home, He told him not to tell us how wonderful it is; we'd probably be too anxious to get there to concentrate on our daily work on this earth!

Scripture References: Matthew 6:10; Luke 11:2.

Q. 113. What do we pray for in the second petition?
A. *That the Gospel may be preached in all the world, and believed and obeyed by us and all men,*

What does this have to do with the second coming? The Scriptures say Christ is not coming until the Gospel has been preached to all men. We pray that this will happen soon. In praying this, what are we doing? We are praying that He might send some of us to the mission field. We are giving to Him all of the children in this church if He chooses to take them. We are asking that the Gospel will be preached in all the world, so that Christ will come and receive us into glory. We've learned how wonderful Heaven is, and now we learn that the way to hasten Jesus' coming for us is to get busy and tell the Gospel to everyone. This means not only that every child should pray that the Lord will send him or her to the mission field if He so chooses, but also that each child should feel constrained to share the Gospel with all with whom he or she comes in contact, at every opportunity. Read to them from Ezekiel 33:3-8 and following, and explain what our Lord is saying to us. This is what it means for us to ask Him to hasten the coming of His kingdom.

Scripture References: Psalm 51:18; Romans 10:1; Colossians 1:28; II Thessalonians 3:1; II Peter 3:11-13.

Q. 114. What is the third petition?
A. _"Thy will be done in earth, as it is in Heaven."_

Did He promise this? He promises that His will is done on earth in accordance with the yieldedness of the Christian. The Holy Spirit works God's will in your life through your yieldedness to God. Ephesians 3:20 says, "...and now unto Him who is able to do abundantly above all we can ask or think _according to the power that worketh in us,_ be glory and honor, dominion and power both now and forever." God is going to have His will in my life, and He will either work through my yieldedness or He will work through my stubbornness, in which case I go through much more fire. He has to burn much more dross. I will have many more hard times, heartaches, and disappointments, but He is going to accomplish His will in my life. So we pray that His will be done on this earth. How? Just as it is done in Heaven. The angels don't hesitate a moment to do God's will. Remind the children that there are hosts of angels in Heaven who do God's will. There are some angels whose job it is to guard the holiness of God; there are some who fight at His command (as Elijah saw all around him). Some are the Lord's messengers, and some protect God's children. It is interesting to think about the many thousands of angels and their many jobs, but we know for *sure* that when God calls one to do His bidding, that angel doesn't say, "Wait just a minute!" The angels obey God *immediately*.

Scripture References: Matthew 6:10; Luke 11:2.

Q. 115. What do we pray for in the third petition?
A. *That men on earth may serve God as the angels do in Heaven.*

Perhaps the best way to teach Questions 114 and 115 is together. Teach the answers to both questions. Then give the above explanation.

Scripture References: Psalm 103:20-22; Psalm 110:34-36; Acts 21:14.

Q. 116. What is the fourth petition?
A. *"Give us this day our daily bread."*

Most of our children don't believe this is necessary, for they are fully confident that they are going to have supper when they get home from catechism class. It has never entered their minds that Daddy will not provide enough money for Mother to buy groceries. They know that there will be something in the refrigerator, and even if there is no food cooked they can find enough to eat. If Mother gets sick and is taken to the hospital, there is still food in the house. So they don't really pray this and mean it, and we don't either. We don't really think that eveything that we have comes from God. We owe Him thanks for every meal that we have. We should stop and consider this and know that every good and perfect gift comes from above. He provides and He is the one who can take it all away. He can suddenly move it with a cyclone or tornado. There are many people who have discovered they don't have food for tonight. We don't pray for the kind of food that you are accustomed to having, but just for sustenance, enough to keep the body today. (If any have read John Noble's books, **I Was a Slave in Russia** and **I Found God in Russia,** they will remember that in the slave camp he went so many days without food or water, claiming this promise that God would give him enough to keep him alive. The Lord did supply his food but not until he was so weak he could only crawl to his cell door for his daily cup of water.) We may not get our wants, but God promises to provide our needs. We will not always get jelly, lemon pie, or steak, but we will get the food necessary for our bodies. (An abundance of Vitamin C is in wild rose hips and violet leaves. Grass is nutritious and should be included in our daily diet, according to some nutritionists. Many weeds are nutritious. Nebuchadnezzar existed on grass in the fields three years. The abundance of God's provision for our needs staggers the imagination.) What, then, is the reason for this petition? We pray that our needs and God's provisions will meet in His perfect timing.

Scripture References: Matthew 6:11; Luke 11:3.

Q. 117. What do we pray for in the fourth petition?
A. *That God would give us all things needful for our bodies and souls.*

Be sure the group understands that "needful" means those things that are necessary, not just desired. This also includes Christ, the bread of life, sufficient for all our spiritual needs as well. We may come to the well of the water of life and drink deeply, for He will never turn off the source or say, "That's enough."

Scripture References: Proverbs 10:22; 30:8; Matthew 6:25-33; Luke 12:22-31; Philippians 4:19; I Timothy 4:4-5.

Q. 118. What is the fifth petition?
A. *"And forgive us our debts, as we forgive our debtors."*

"Debts" and "debtors" are words to be explained. "Debts" means those things that we owe. The word "trespasses" is used in Matthew. Christ says if we forgive not men their trespasses neither will our Heavenly Father forgive us our trespasses. That means the things that we have done wrong. We are taught here forgiveness, and we are taught to ask God to forgive us.

Scripture References: Psalm 51:1; Matthew 6:12,14-15; Luke 11:4; Revelation 3:24-25.

Q. 119. What do we pray for in the fifth petition?
A. *That God would pardon our sins for Christ's sake, and enable us to forgive those who have injured us.*

Why don't we want to pardon the person who has injured us? Because we are afraid that he will get by with the offense. We are afraid that if we forgive him, God will forgive him, too, and he will get by. We want him to be punished! We are afraid that God will treat him just as He treats us. He forgives us, but we don't want Him to treat the other person that way. The wording of this does not mean that my forgiveness is based on my ability to forgive others. That would be works. I am saved by belief in Christ who forgives my sins. I am not saved through a work of forgiveness. However, my forgiving spirit is the fruit or proof of my salvation, or God's having forgiven me; while an unforgiving spirit may well be the proof of my having never received God's forgiveness! I grow spiritually by asking Him to enable me to forgive the other fellow just as He forgave me. How? He has hidden my sins. He remembers them no more against me. Now through sanctification He teaches me and enables me to forgive the other fellow the same way. In this question we have to explain "pardon" and "injured." This makes this question clearer to children. "Pardon" is forgiveness and "injured" means those who have sinned against or wronged us, hurt our feelings or our physical bodies.

It is important to teach the children *how* to forgive, rather than just to require it of them. In this petition we pray that God would *enable* us to forgive others. But we don't wait until we feel forgiveness to exercise forgiveness. According to Romans 6:11, we commit to the Lord our unforgiving spirits and by faith forgive as an act of the will in obedience to His commands, trusting Him to produce the feeling later. Remind them of the times Mother made them hug a sibling or friend and apologize. They didn't *feel* like apologizing, but an act of *obedience* resulted soon in absolute and complete forgiveness, and they were soon ready to play again, all offenses forgotten. It is thus with our Lord's dealings with us. He will give the strength to obey His word, but sometimes it still takes all we have to complete the act.

Scripture References: Psalm 51:1; Romans 3:24-25.

Q. 120. What is the sixth petition?
A. *"And lead us not into temptation, but deliver us from evil."*

We should go back to Question number 32 here. Who tempted them to this sin? The devil tempted Eve and she gave the fruit to Adam. We are praying that the devil will not tempt us beyond that we are able. Who led Jesus into the wilderness to be tempted of the devil? The Bible says the Holy Spirit led Jesus. Here we have to explain temptation. Temptation is two-fold. God tempted Abraham when He led him up the mountain to sacrifice Isaac. In that sense it means "tested." When the *devil* tempts us it means "tries to make us do wrong." The Bible says, "Let no man say that he is tempted of God, for God tempts no man." Yet the Bible says that He tempted Abraham. What does it mean? Our Lord does not try to make anyone commit sin, but God *tested* Abraham. Why does He do this? He is burning out the dross. He is purifying the silver. We don't grow in Christ if we are not tested. I Peter says, "Let him not be ashamed when he is tried by some trial. Blessed is the man who endures temptation for he comes out of it a better Christian."

Think about it. If I were never tempted, never had to choose between right and wrong, from whence would I derive my strength? God promises that there shall no temptation come to you, but that He will give you the power to overcome. That is a promise that we have to claim often. God allows the Holy Spirit to lead us into a place of tempting. God does not put the temptation in front of us and tempt us to do wrong. The devil tempts us to sin. God allows the tempting and allows us to be put in that position where the devil tempts us. The devil is one of God's instruments. God uses the devil to tempt us and then He gives us the strength to overcome the temptation. The devil is not stronger than God. He can't tempt us to do anything that God cannot keep us from doing. God says, "I can keep you from yielding to any temptation. You don't ever have to do what the devil tempts you to do. I will let him tempt you, but that is for My glory. That is so you will grow." But we feel afraid. We say, "Don't lead me into temptation." Why? "Because I am not strong enough and I will forget to call on You and I will fall into that temptation and I will do what the devil tells me to do. I have done it so many times. Lord, I am so weak. Don't lead me into the temptation." What we are saying is, "Deliver us from temptation." We are saying, "Be merciful. Don't lead me into any more testing than I will be given the grace to overcome." We are confessing our weaknesses and claiming His mercy.

Scripture References: Matthew 6:13; Luke 11:4.

Q. 121. What do we pray for in the sixth petition?
A. *That God would keep us from sin.*

That is what we are asking. We know that the Holy Spirit is going to lead us into places of testing, and we are asking that He will keep us from yielding to the devil.

Scripture References: Psalm 19:13; Psalm 51:10; Matthew 26:41; I Corinthians 10:13.

Q. 122. How many sacraments are there?
A. *Two.*

Although the Confession of Faith and the Larger and Shorter
Catechisms give the definition of a sacrament, the question "What
is a sacrament?" and its answer do not appear in the Child's
Catechism. Try to answer this question in order for the children to
understand it as much as possible.

A sacrament is an outward, holy sign or seal instituted or begun
by Christ which testifies to the application of the covenant of grace
to believers. The sacrament is an outward act which signifies what
has happened in the heart. Refer to Questions 43-45 and 49-51 to
review the covenant of grace, (which was an agreement between
God the Father and God the Son, that Christ would come to earth
to keep the whole law for His people and suffer the punishment
due to their sins; and God the Father would forgive those for whom
Christ should die, and treat them as if they had never sinned,
making them holy in heart and conduct). A sign points to
something. A sacrament, then, is something that points to the
salvation and sanctification that are ours through the covenant of
grace.

A seal is a stamp of approval or authentication. The government's seal on a document means that document is official.
Therefore a person who receives a sacrament accepts it as the
authorized and official outward act representing the appropriation
to his/her own life of the benefits of the covenant of grace.

When you receive a certificate of graduation from Bible school,
the seal on it means that this certificate is official, that you really
did come regularly and do the work to graduate. It seals and points
to something that's been done already. When we salute the
American flag, this is an outward act that testifies to or points to our
citizenship in this country. Our saluting the flag does not make us
citizens of America, but points to something that has already been
done, and to a citizenship we already enjoy. This is not called a
sacrament because it was not an outward act designed or decreed
by God in the New Testament just for believers. When someone
puts on a Scout uniform this is an outward symbol pointing to the

fact that he belongs to that organization and conducts himself by
their laws and believes in those things for which they stand. But
putting on the uniform does not **MAKE** one a Scout. It is only an
outward sign pointing to the fact that he is already a Scout. It is not
a sacrament because Christ did not start it, but this should help us
understand what a sacrament is.

There are only two of these signs and seals, or outward acts,
instigated (instituted or begun) in the New Testament. Create
some interest in and enthusiasm for these two signs, by seeing if the
children can guess what they are. You can make it fun for them by
asking, "What do you think you could do as an outward sign to let
people know that you accept the covenant of grace for yourself —
that is, that you believe Christ died for you, and you have given
your heart to Him? Would you wear a red cardboard heart on your
collar, or a cross necklace? Would you walk around all the time
with your hands folded in prayer? What do you think Christ
thought would be a good way to point to or seal your belief in
Him?" This is a good way to introduce the next question.

Scripture Reference: I Corinthians 11:23-29.
See Also: Shorter Catechism 93; Larger Catechism 164, Confession
of Faith 29:4; 30:1; 31:1-8. The Confession of Faith should be
studied carefully before teaching the sacraments. It gives the
scriptural bases also.

Q. 123. What are they?
A. *Baptism and the Lord's supper.*

We help the children to see that if and when a person has been
regenerated and truly given his/her life to the Lord, he will want to
commit the outward act of uniting with a church, to show to the
world and to the Christian community what the Lord has done for
him and in him. We have talked about the importance of
presenting the Plan of Salvation to the children in prayerful hope
that some will make a commitment to Jesus Christ as Lord of their
lives. I think it is also important to talk to them about church
membership. The child who has truly claimed Christ as Saviour

should be ready publicly to profess Him before men, and unite with the body of believers. All too often the parents seem reluctant to discuss this matter with the children, wanting the decision to be wholly theirs. This is one reason we should discuss it and teach it in catechism classes. Some adult needs to explain to the children the importance of church affiliation as a part of their public profession, and joining the body of believers in Christ.

I do not think it is a mistake to teach the children the difference in our beliefs on the sacraments, and those of other faiths. Our children sometimes grow up and marry into other faiths because they've never been told the differences. The questions on the sacraments give us an excellent opportunity to teach the differences in Protestantism and Catholicism. The Catholics observe seven sacraments. They have "Marriage" as a sacrament; "Baptism" of babies, as we do; then "Confirmation" (a person accepting for himself as a sacrament); "Penance," that is doing something to get forgiveness. (They confess to the priest and he absolves them. He can grant them forgiveness, for they believe that the keys of Heaven were handed down to him and that he has the ability to grant them forgiveness, in the name of Christ; but they are to do certain things that will show that they are sorry, and merit that forgiveness.) "Orders" is a sacrament that has to do with becoming monks or nuns, or separatists from other people, a practice the Bible specifically condemns. Then there is "Extreme Unction" which is the last rites at death. Their other two are the same as ours, the Lord's Supper and baptism. We don't find a basis for their other sacraments. Some denominations say that baptism is necessary, and that if the person who administers the Lord's Supper and baptism is right with God, then it becomes salvation to us. There again we are most concerned for our Catholic friends, who believe that if this child is baptized, he is baptized into the kingdom of Heaven. The missionaries to Spain and Portugal and other Catholic countries, who ask some of the natives, "Are you a Christian?" tell us they will say, "Oh yes, I was baptized into the church on a certain date." In their minds they are baptized into the body of Christ. Then the missionary asks, "Do you know Christ as your Saviour?" They say, "Oh no." They don't know about that, but they were accepted into the kingdom because the priest's attitude was right. He was God's representative, and he ushered them in. So there is a great ministry to the Catholic who believes that he is saved through the church. I have heard people say they had Catholic friends who were saved, for they had put their trust in Christ as their Saviour. That is fine! But if they have put their trust in the church (and that is the Catholic teaching), and the church's ability to usher them into the kingdom, they are lost. They don't need our condemnation; nobody who is lost merits our condemnation, but they need our love, and our witness and our testimony, and the truth. Remember Ephesians says to give them the truth in love. We are commanded to love these people. The children should be taught the difference in Catholicism and Protestantism. They should be taught not to look down on the person who is a Catholic. He may be a much better citizen than we are and make more of a contribution to this world than we do. Our attitude is of love and compassion. We know the truth of salvation and we owe it to anybody in the world who does not have it. All of the children need to know what sacraments are and what they mean and what is involved.

For the little children, explain what the Lord's Supper is, for often they do not know. It is the passing and partaking of bread and wine in church.

Baptism and the Lord's Supper are the only two sacraments we've been told specifically by Christ to celebrate. These are the only two outward acts that Christ requires of us as believers, as signs pointing to our union with Him through the covenant of grace.

In the Old Testament God instituted circumcision as the sign and seal of His covenant with His people. The believer was to receive the outward act, or sign and seal of circumcision, testifying to his belief in the covenantal promises of God. Baptism in the New Testament takes the place of circumcision in the Old. Also in the Old Testament, the Passover Feast was instituted by God for His people, commemorating their deliverance from bondage through the shed blood of the lamb. In the New Testament, the Lord's Supper takes the place of the Passover Feast, as Christ is our

Passover, the Lamb of God sacrificed for us to take away the sin of the world.

References: See References for Question 122.

Q. 124. Who appointed these sacraments?
A. *The Lord Jesus Christ.*

"Appointed" means started them. He started them and He was the one who said to do them, and that is the reason we observe them. In discussing Question 123 you will have children who are not taking the Lord's Supper for they are not members of the church, and there may be some who do not go to church. Explain to them what baptism is. It is the sprinkling of the water on the head or the immersing of the body into the water.

They will have little Baptist friends who believe that immersion is the only way to baptize. Anticipate these questions. They should know that Scripture says we are buried in baptism with Christ and are raised up again into the new life with Him. This is the Scripture upon which the Baptists base immersion. They believe that one must be completely buried. The old man is buried and the new man is raised. We believe in sprinkling. We base the sprinkling on the descending of the dove at Christ's baptism and the tongues of fire at Pentecost and the sprinkling of the congregation in the Old Testament. Christ said, "Ye will be baptized with the Holy Spirit not many days hence." And when He left, the Holy Spirit descended on their heads as tongues of fire. Our symbol is the sprinkling of water on the head.

Remember that a symbol is the outward sign of the inward act. The water is used because it is nature's method of cleansing. Salvation is a cleansing. In the Lord's Supper bread and wine are used as types of nourishment. Just as water is a type of cleansing, the bread and wine are types of nourishment of our souls, and spiritual growth demonstrated, as we take more of the spirit of Christ into our hearts. Excellent pamphlets to read in this connection are: **BAPTISM BY SPRINKLING,** by Ben Lacy Rose, published by the Presbyterian Journal; **WHY WE BAPTIZE BY**

SPRINKLING, by J.B. Green, published by the Presbyterian Journal.

Scripture References: Matthew 28:18-20; I Corinthians 11:24-26.

Q. 125. Why did Christ appoint these sacraments?
A. *To distinguish His disciples from the world, and to comfort and strengthen them.* (This is an important answer.)

That means that they are different. These are ways that the Christian shows the world that he is different. He has been baptized and he partakes of the Lord's Supper. ("Distinguish" means to set apart as different.)

"Comfort" means to make one feel better. Mother "comforts" us when we have been hurt. The Lord's Supper and baptism are given to us as a comfort. They clinch or seal. The Bible calls it a seal. It makes us know that we are children of God. There will be doubts, but at the time we accept Him, we believe to the extent that we are willing to be baptized, and we take the Lord's Supper, and these encourage our Christian lives. They help us when we are down; they comfort us in times of stress and sorrow; they remind us that we are God's children and that we are growing on the nourishment of Christ; and they strengthen us. He says do these things "as oft as ye do them in remembrance of Me." It is good to come to church every Sunday and be busy with our church work, but it is good to be brought back periodically to the table of communion, and to partake again of the blood and body of Christ. They are to strengthen us.

Scripture References: Romans 9:8; I Corinthians 10:16-17,21; I Corinthians 11:27-29; Galatians 3:27,29; Galatians 6:15.

Q. 126. What sign is used in baptism?
A. *The washing with water.*

We have talked about the fact that sacraments are signs, and the sign of baptism is the washing with water. Water is a sign that we have accepted Christ and have been washed in His blood, and are new creatures.

Scripture References: John 3:5; Ephesians 5:26.

Q. 127. What does this signify?
A. *That we are cleansed from sin by the blood of Christ.*

What does this mean? To what does this sign point? "Sign" means that it points to something, and this sign points to the fact that I am cleansed by the blood of Christ. "Cleansed" means cleaned. Children know the difference in getting into the tub and playing, and getting into the tub and washing themselves clean! We are cleansed from sin, washed clean from sin by the blood of Christ. Remind the children that the human heart is the only thing that starts out black and can be washed in red and turn out white. That is the story of what Christ does to our hearts when we commit our lives to Him. He washed them in the blood of Christ, and when the Father looks at us He doesn't see sin, for He is looking at our hearts through the blood of Christ. The Bible tells us that we are washed as white as snow. There is nothing we can do that will not be covered by the blood of Christ.

Scripture References: I Corinthians 6:11; Colossians 2:11-12; Titus 3:5.

Q. 128. In whose name are we baptized?
A. *In the name of the Father, and of the Son, and of the Holy Ghost.*

The cross reference is to the questions on the Trinity, Questions 7 and 8. In how many persons does this one God exist? And what are they? The Father, Son and the Holy Ghost. We have already laid the foundation, and as we progress deeper into doctrine, there will be less explaining, for the boys and girls are building on what you have already given them. Here we are building on the doctrine of the Trinity, and there again we sing each Sunday the Doxology, "Praise God from whom all blessings flow....Praise Father, Son and Holy Ghost." We are taught to praise the Holy Ghost for what He is doing in our lives, praise the Son for what He has done for us, and praise the Father for bringing all of this about. We are to praise in the name of all three, and we are to baptize in the name of all three.

Scripture Reference: Matthew 28:19-20.
Cf. Questions: 7,8.

Q. 129. Who are to be baptized?
A. Believers and their children.

I open my classes to any child who wants to come. All children are invited. Each time we have Baptist children to visit, when I get to Questions 122 and 129, I tell them, "This is the way we believe and this is the way we teach. Your parents do not believe this way; but take this Catechism we give you and show your parents how we teach. It is a point of doctrine, but not a point of salvation. I don't mind teaching them, but I want their parents to know that we are teaching a Scriptural point with which they disagree. The Scriptures are in Acts 2:38-39, Acts 16:31-34, and I Corinthians 7:14. Believers and their children should be baptized. In Acts Paul, speaking to the Philippian jailer says, "Believe on the Lord Jesus Christ and you shall be saved and your house." How many times the promise is "to you and your house." "The promise" — Genesis 17 — what promise was given to Abraham and his children, with the seal performed in the baby? The adult who became converted to the Jewish faith was circumcised, but the baby born into the line received the sign of the promise also. The covenant children are the children of believing parents.

We are accused of believing that our children are going to heaven because we are Christians. We don't believe that. We believe they are going to heaven because of the covenant relationship in which God promised to be a God to the children of believers. We have to claim this promise. God put the children in a Christian home as a part of His plan. He also requires proper biblical training of the child.

Our Book of Church Order includes the following questions to the parents as a part of our service of baptism of infants. "Do you acknowledge your child's need of the cleansing blood of Jesus Christ, and the renewing grace of the Holy Spirit? Do you claim God's covenant promises in (his) behalf, and do you look in faith to the Lord Jesus Christ for (his) salvation, as you do for your own? Do you now unreservedly dedicate your child to God, and promise in humble reliance upon divine grace, that you will endeavor to set before (him) a Godly example, that you will pray with and for (him), that you will teach (him) the doctrines of our holy religion, and that you will strive, by all the means of God's appointment, to bring (him) up in the nurture and admonition of the Lord?" The congregation are also challenged to heed their responsibility as a part of the body of Christ to assist the parents in the Christian nurture of this child.

The late Dr. Peter Eldersveld of "The Back to God Hour" broadcast, in speaking about the ecumenical movement, said, "Suppose a friend and I go talk to a man about total commitment to Christ, and he accepts Christ as Lord and Saviour in his life, and is baptized, and we both welcome him into the kingdom of God. Then the friend says, 'Let's go to another.' and I say, 'Wait a minute, what about this man's children? I want to baptize those children.' Then the friend says, 'But they haven't repented.' So here we'd part ways."

The Presbyterians believe that baptism is the sign of our belief in something already promised by God. Some of our Christian brethren from other denominations believe it is **MAN'S RE-SPONSE** to God's offer. This is why they cannot baptize infants, because infants cannot repent. But we can baptize infants because we come in faith appropriating the promise of a redemption already purchased by someone outside of ourselves. Presbyterians believe we are to bring the children for baptism because they are children of the promise. I have the utmost faith that every one of my children will be saved. Since teaching this course several years ago all of our children have made personal commitments to Jesus Christ as Lord and Saviour of their lives.) If you make a personal commitment to Christ, you should claim this covenant promise for your children also. God did not say that all our children would be sweet and nice and we'd never have any trouble with any of them. He said that the promise of salvation is to "you and your house." You will be saved, and your house. Let's look at I Corinthians 7:14 for your own background. Paul talks about marriage and not being unevenly joined to unbelievers. What about two who are married and *then* one of them accepts Christ? Does the Christian leave the non-Christian? No, you are under an obligation to stay and live the Christian life. The husband is sanctified by the wife and the wife is sanctified by the husband, *else were their children unclean*. The unsaved parent may not ever be saved, but the saved parent can claim the covenant promise for the sake of the children.

Scripture References: Acts 2:38-39; 16:31-34; I Corinthians 7:14.

Q. 130. Why should infants be baptized?
A. *Because they have a sinful nature and need a Saviour.*

What is baptism? It is a sign by the washing of water that we are cleansed from sin by the blood of Christ. Some day that child will have to come to the point of making his own confession and profession. Dr. Eldersveld said he could never remember the time he did not thank the Lord at night that he was one of His children, for he had been taught that he was a covenant child. Then the time came when he wanted to make his own profession of faith. He realized that he was a sinner; he received the promise as an undeserved favor of God and he joined the church. But long before that he knew that he was a child of God.

I was asked one night, "Just how have you taught your children this?" I replied that we had altered our teaching as we grew spiritually. The older ones were taught that they must accept Christ. We are teaching the little ones that they are children of the covenant and God loves them, but they are sinners and must come to the Lord. The older ones did not have the advantage of the covenant teaching because we did not know it and did not give it to them. We are explaining to the little ones the covenant promise and I also explain to them their need for a Saviour. They need to accept the Saviour for themselves.

Baptism is a sign, and we give it to our children because they have a sinful nature. Here you go into Questions 34 through 38 which are about needing a Saviour, that our hearts must be changed before they can be fit for Heaven. Question 42, "Why can none be saved through the covenant of works?" "Because all have broken it." Question 70 is: "Why do you need Christ as a priest?" "Because I am guilty." Go back and review all of those questions. We have a sinful nature. Where did we get it? We inherited it from Adam for he represented all his posterity.

Scripture References: Genesis 8:21; Romans 3:23,10,12; James 2:10. **Cf. Questions:** 34-38,42,70.

Q. 131. Does Christ care for little children?

A. Yes; for he says, "Suffer the little children to come unto me, and forbid them not; for of such is the kingdom of God."

Now go to Question 129 and explain "believers" to them. The catechism rarely uses the word believers. The righteous, the pious, the Christians are those who believe unto salvation. They are the saved people. In Question 130 explain "sinful nature." Remind them of that original sin. Your nature means that you are made up like that. Many people say, "I have a horrible disposition and blow up easily," and they name all of their defects, then excuse them by saying, "But this is just my nature." They are not to be excused as natural, however. They are to be recognized as evidence of a sinful nature which must be dealt with, confessed, cleansed and sanctified. We are to want to be like Christ in all things. In Question 131 explain "suffer." It means allow or let. Often third graders don't know what suffer means. We have already talked about transgressions and the things that God has forbidden in His law. Remind the children here that "forbids" means to say not to. "Transgression" is doing what God forbids. Don't "forbid the children to come unto Me" means don't tell them not to, or that they mustn't or can't. Our Lord says the Kingdom of God is made of people who have a simple faith just like a little child.

Scripture References: Matthew 19:13-14; Mark 10:13-16; Luke 18:15-16.

Q. 132. To what does your baptism bind you?
A. *To be a true follower of Christ.*

That means that since we now have Christ as Lord and Saviour, we are to live as children of His.

Scripture References: Romans 6:4; Galatians 3:26-27.

Q. 133. What is the Lord's supper?
A. *The eating of bread and drinking of wine in remembrance of the sufferings and death of Christ.*

What does "remembrance" mean? It means to remember. The Lord's Supper reminds us of these things and makes us appreciate our salvation. We always need to go back and look at the cross, and the Lord's Supper helps us to do that. Taking the elements is also a reminder of the indwelling of the Holy Spirit to empower us, sent after Christ ascended to Heaven.

Scripture Reference: I Corinthians 11:26.

Q. 134. What does the bread represent?
A. *The body of Christ, broken for our sins.*

a high priest who was tempted in all points like as we are yet without sin. He is in Heaven interceding for us, and "interceding" means praying for us. Sinners are those who are still doing wrong, and that includes all of us, but Christ is reminding God of the covenant of grace. "I died for her and I am pleading that she come to Heaven anyway, because I died for her, and My blood is sufficient to pay for her sins."

Scripture References: Romans 8:34; Hebrews 4:14-16.

Q. 139. Will He come again?
A. Yes; at the last day Christ will come to judge the world.

This last page is about eternal life. This is where we get into all of the beautiful Scriptures on the second coming of Christ. In Thessalonians it is said that the sky will part and the trumpet will sound and Christ will come with a shout. Everybody will see Him and know it is Christ. The saved will know that this is our Lord and we will meet Him in the air. The unsaved will see Him and know that He is God and that this is the God they rejected. There will be no split decisions once that sky is opened. It is finished then. So we should have a concern for those people who don't know their salvation to turn to Christ today, for there might not be a tomorrow. Christ said that God did not even tell Him when it would take place. We can see the signs of the times and know that we are in the last days, but we don't know the exact time. Nobody knows this. He will come for what? To judge the world. Give references to the children to look up and make it clear that His purpose for coming is not to judge whether or not I am saved though He will pronounce that for the world to know. None of you know whether or not I am saved, for you don't know my heart, but some day the whole world will know. The saved will go on His right hand and the unsaved on His left. He will separate them. He says that He will separate the wheat from the chaff in the last day. This does not mean that I won't know that I am saved. We can know now if we are saved. It is the teaching of some people that we

don't know until Judgment Day, but we can know now whether we've committed our lives to Christ. "These accepted me and these rejected me. These will be judged for the deeds done in the flesh, to determine the reward."
We will be rewarded on that day. He says there will be many deeds you did that will be burned. Maybe you thought that these were good works, but they were not good and they will be burned, but you will be saved so as by fire. At that time there will be an accounting of our deeds done in the flesh and whether or not we receive any rewards. But our sins were judged on Calvary. Our salvation was determined a long time ago.

Scripture References: Acts 17:31; Romans 2:16; Revelation 20:12.

Q. 140. What becomes of men at death?
A. The body returns to dust, and the soul goes into the world of spirits.

That is why it is important on the first page to teach the children that they are made from dust, because you tell them that they go back to dust. The Scriptures are in Job and Psalms that the body turns to dust and the soul goes into the world of spirits. There are many ways they could get off on this world of spirits, but if we can keep them excited over Heaven, that is the main point on this page. What is Heaven? That is where the soul goes immediately. The soul or spirit is there, but the body will rise someday, and will become united with the soul.

Scripture References: Psalm 90:5-6.

Q. 141. Will the bodies of the dead be raised to life again?
A. Yes; "the trumpet shall sound, and the dead shall be raised."

The Bible tells us that the dead in Christ will be raised first and those of us who are living will rise with them. Many children do not know that the body is going to be resurrected. Then they will get off on what it is going to be like. Will we recognize each other? If you teach them that we recognize each other, then somebody will worry about a father or relative who is not saved. And they are going to think that they will not be completely happy, "Because I know a person that I love is not going to be there, and I am going to miss him." This is bringing Heaven down to man's ability to understand, and man's emotions. In Heaven we will recognize each other as Christians, but the Bible also says there will be no tears, and there will be no sorrow. So when we get to Heaven and understand all things and know as we are known and see our deeds done in the flesh and see what terrible sinners we were, (for we don't know now how bad we are and we think that we are better than God knows we are), when we see what kind of people we were and He loved us and saved us, we are going to see that anybody not there deserved damnation. We are not going to be grieved over that, for being filled with the joy of what we have!

It is wrong for us to say that God is so inadequate that He could take us to a Heaven we wouldn't like. We have to believe that Heaven is a glorious place. This is the triumphal note on which we end. We are taught in the Scriptures that we will have glorified bodies, and it is said that they will be like the angels'. (I was taught that angels were sexless, but since then I have found that it is more nearly correct that they are male since they are referred to as "he" and are given male names.) There will be no marriage or giving in marriage in Heaven. The children should be reminded that the little fellow that is deformed or crippled or wearing glasses will not have those imperfections in Heaven. His body will be perfect and he will not be bound by the means of transportation that we have on this earth. Everything will be wonderful. Those of us who live so long that we have false teeth and can't get around and everything about us is wearing out — well, that is not going to be so in Heaven, for we will have glorified bodies that will be perfect.

John said that God told him not to write what he saw in Heaven. Why? Because we would be so impatient to get there this earth would seem awful to us. Let these children know that it is better than anything they ever had or ever will have on this earth.

Scripture Reference: I Thessalonians 4:16.

Q. 142. What will become of the wicked in the day of judgment?
A. *They shall be cast into hell.*

"Cast" means thrown. They will be thrown into Hell. The
Scripture says that they will be thrown into the lake of fire with the
devil and his angels.

Scripture References: Revelation 20:15; 21:8,27.

Q. 143. What is hell?
A. *A place of dreadful and endless torment.*

Don't let these children feel pity for the person that is in Hell. We
attempt to judge God, for we think Hell is an awful punishment for
God to inflict on anyone. We forget that we deserve it. Our sins are
so awful we deserve Hell. If a person had been in Hell ten years and
then was given the opportunity to go to Heaven, what would he
say? He would let out the worst string of oaths known to man,
because of his hatred for God, and his rejection of Him. Nothing
about Hell would make him like God, it would just make him hate
God worse. (I had always thought that if those people just had one
half a chance they would accept God and go to Heaven.) These
people may desire the things of ease and comfort, but they don't
desire the things of Heaven. God, the sovereign, merciful,
wonderful, loving Heavenly Father who protects us, loves us and
humbles us, has given us the ability to love Him in a small way. Yet
when we get to Heaven we are going to be able to love Him fully.
On some occasions we feel that we could burst with our love for
Him. We will not feel like that in Heaven for we will be able to
express our love for Him completely. The people in Hell don't
have it and they don't want it. Just be careful that the children don't
think that God is hard and mean, for we run into that
misconception the rest of our life. (My husband and I talked to a

man older than we are the other day who is openly agnostic, and all that he would say was that he could not accept a God who would condemn people who had never heard of Him.) We hear it over and over: What about the fellow who never heard of Him? These people are judging God. He says, "Your ways are not my ways. You do not understand why I do as I do. You won't understand until you get to Heaven. Then you will see face to face and you will know as you are known." But people reject God because He does things they don't understand. Let's not plant that idea in the mind of the child. Find the Scriptures where Christ talks about Hell. He says that it is a horrible place. What is Hell? It is a place of dreadful and endless torment. "Dreadful" means horrible, terrible, and "torment" means punishment and anguish and suffering. "Torment" is hurting badly, and that is how it is going to be in Hell forever. Christ talks about it, and some have said that He talked as much about Hell as anything else.

Scripture References: Matthew 3:12; 5:22; 10:28; 18:9; Mark 9:43,47-48; Luke 16:23; II Peter 2:4.

Q. 144. What will become of the righteous?
A. *They shall be taken to heaven.*

Explain "righteous." We use different words every time we talk about the Christian. "Righteous" means you are right. How did I get to be right? Because the rightness of Christ is imputed to me. Children won't know what that means, that I am seen as right by God because the rightness of Christ is given to me. That is another way of saying that my sins were not only washed away, for if my sins were washed away and that was all that was left, I would be white, but I would be a white nothing. This is true for there is no good in me, so the good of Christ is imputed or given to me. The best way to do it is to use black and white chalk and write "Christ" in white, and "Me" in black. Then draw arrows across showing His righteousness in white and my black sins put on Him. Thus we swap places. God condemns Him to death for what? His white righteousness? No, for the black sins that were put on Him. So I live in Heaven forever as a saint. Why? For my black sins? No, for the white righteousness of Christ that was given to me. Now we live in Heaven not only because He washed my bad, but He gave to me His good.

Illustration

CHRIST   ME

RIGHTEOUS   SIN

WHITE   BLACK

This is what righteous means, and explains who the righteous are. They shall be taken to Heaven. This is the most triumphant note. Can you conceive of a more wonderful note on which to close this catechism?

Scripture References: John 14:2-3; I Thessalonians 4:17; I Peter 1:4; Revelation 21:27.

Q. 145. What is heaven?
A. A glorious and happy place, where the righteous shall be forever with the LORD.

What are we going to do in Heaven? The Bible teaches that we are going to praise God forever. When we grow in our love for Christ to the extent that we fully realize what kind of people we are, and that nothing but the grace of God saved us and got us to this place (which is so wonderful that words could not describe it and we are not allowed to see into it), we will praise Him forever. We'll love Him so much that we will never tire of telling Him how much we love Him, for the rest of time. Revelation 21 gives a description of Heaven. Read to them of the gates of pearl, the streets of gold and the foundation of jasper. (If you could get pictures from a jeweler to let them know just what these stones are it will help to bring the beauty to the child. I took crayons and colored the different things mentioned in the nearest shade possible.) It is going to be indescribable. It is going to be the most beautiful, most wonderful place ever. It is going to be more wonderful than anything we have ever seen. The glory in question there — what was the little fellow's definition of glory? All he could remember was the brightness, and here it is, so the definition was not so far off after all. There is no night there. It will be as bright as the noonday sun. It is a glorious and happy place where those of us who have trusted Christ as Lord of our lives will be forever with the Lord.

If we would teach this catechism, (and the only way that we can do it is with the Lord's help), I think it is one of the greatest things we could do for our children. It will show them what salvation can mean to their eternal destiny, and what our eternal destiny is. We love this world. We think this is a nice world. We have not begun to realize the glories of Heaven. Paul says, "For to me to live is Christ," as long as I am on this earth, my job is to tell the world about Christ. "But to die is gain." That is going to be my day! And what a tragedy that we Christians put on black, and show to the world that we have no wonderful Heaven when we have a funeral. We observe our funerals just like the pagans. We seldom allow a Christian life to end on a triumphant note. It will be the greatest day of my life! I will go to Heaven and it should be a triumph. I have seen some funerals where the family wore white and the Doxology was sung and it was a praise to the Lord. "This saint's gone home!" There are no more worries, no more sorrows, no more tears, pain, or night, and it is a glorious and happy place, where the righteous will be forever with the Lord!

Scripture References: John 14:2-3; Revelation 21:1-4,18-25.

BIBLE REFERENCES

1. Gen. 1:27; 5:2; Job 33:4; Psl. 100:3; Isa. 44:2a; 51:13; Mal. 2:10; Acts 17:28.

2. Job 26:13; 33:4; Psl. 33:6-7; John 1:1,3; Acts 17:24-25; I Cor. 8:6; Eph. 3:9; Col. 1:16; Heb. 1:1-2; 11:3.

3. Psl. 19:1; Isa. 43:7; 45:18; Acts 17:26-27; Rev. 4:11.

4. Deut. 26:16; 32:46; I Sam. 15:22; Jer. 7:23; Matt. 5:16; 7:21; Lk. 8:21; John 6:29; 15:8,10; Acts 5:29; Rom. 15:6; I Cor. 6:20.

5. Deut. 6:24; II Ki. 6:17; Psl. 16:1; 23; 34:7; 37:28; 91:4; 121; 125:1; 139:13-16; Pro. 2:8; Dan. 6:22; II Tim. 4:18.

6. Deut. 6:4; Isa. 43:10; 44:6; 45:18; Mk. 12:29; I Cor. 8:4; Eph. 4:4-6; I Tim. 2:5.

7. Matt. 28:19; II Cor. 13:14; I Pet. 1:2; I John 5:7; **Shorter Catechism Question 6**, with proof texts; **Larger Catechism Question 9**, with proof texts; **Confession of Faith Chapter 2:1-3** with proof texts.

8. John 10:30; 14:26; 15:26; 16:28; 17:11; I Cor. 8:6; L.C. 10-11.

9. John 4:24; II Cor. 3:17.

10. Deut. 4:39; Psl. 139:7-12; Isa. 66:1; Jer. 23:23; Acts 17:27.

11. Psl. 139:1-5; Jer. 23:24; Pro. 15:3; John 2:25; Heb. 4:13.

12. Num. 32:23; Psl. 139; Acts 15:18; Heb. 4:13.

13. Gen. 18:14; Psl. 33:11; Isa. 46:10; Matt. 19:26; Mk. 10:27; Lk. 1:37; 18:27; Eph. 1:11; 3:20; Phil. 2:13; Tit. 1:2; Heb. 6:18.

14. Isa. 40:8; Jer. 36:2; Eze. 1:3; John 10:35; 17:17; Acts 1:16; Gal. 1:8-9; II Tim. 3:16; I Pet. 1:25; S.C. 2-3; L.C. 3-5; Con.F. 1:1-10.

15. II Ki. 17:13; Neh. 9:30; Lk. 1:70; Heb. 1:1-2; II Pet. 1:20-21; II Pet. 3:2.

16. Gen. 3:20; Pro. 22:2; Acts 17:26.

17. Gen. 2:7,21-23; 3:19; 18:27; Job 10:9; 34:15; Psl. 103:14; Isa. 40:7-8; I Tim. 2:13; I Pet. 1:24.

18. Gen. 2:7.

19. Job 27:3; Ecc. 12:7; Matt. 10:28; Lk. 12:20; 20:36; John 8:51; 11:26; Acts 17:25; I Cor. 15:54; II Cor. 5:1; Rev. 20:4.

20. Gen. 1:26-27; 9:6; Lk. 20:36; Acts 17:22-23; Rom. 1:19-20; 13:1-4; I Cor. 11:7.

21. Gen. 1:27,31; 2:25; Eph. 4:24.

22. Gen. 9:12; 17:10.

23. Gen. 2:16-17; S.C. 12; L.C. 20; Con.F. 7:1-2.

24. Gen. 2:16-17; Josh. 23:6; Psl. 19:7; Rom. 7:12; Gal. 5:14.

25. Gen. 2:16; 3:22.

26. Gen. 2:17; Eze. 18:20a; John 5:20; Rom. 6:23; Jas. 1:15.

27. Gen. 3:6,17; Rom. 5:12,14,19; I Cor. 15:21-22; I Tim. 2:14; S.C. 13; L.C. 21; Con.F. 6:1-2.

28. Pro. 14:21; 24:9; Rom. 14:23; Jas. 4:17; I Jn. 3:4.

29. Jas. 4:17.

30. I Jn. 3:4.

31. Gen. 2:17; 3:1-6; Cross Reference 16, 30.

32. Gen. 3:1-6; I Tim. 2:14.

33. Gen. 3:16-19,24; Cr. Ref. 2, 21.

34. Rom. 5:12,19; I Cor. 15:22; S.C. 16; L.C. 22; Con.F. 6:3; Cr. Ref. 2, 16.

35. Rom. 5:12,19; I Cor. 15:22; S.C. 17-19; L.C. 23, 25, 26, 27.

36. Rom. 5:12,14-19.

37. Pro. 11:19; John 3:36; Rom. 1:18; 6:23; Gal. 3:10; Eph. 5:6; Heb. 2:2,3.

38. Eze. 36:26; Hab. 1:13; John 1:12-13; 3:3; II Cor. 5:17; I Pet. 1:23; I Jn. 5:1.

39. Tit. 3:5.

40. Lev. 12:12; Neh. 9:20; John 14:26; I Cor. 2:13; 12:3; I Jn. 3:23-24; I Jn. 4:13.

41. Rom. 5:12-19; Gal. 3; 4:24; Eph. 2:8-9.

42. Gen. 6:5; I Ki. 8:46; Psl. 14:1; 53:3; Pro. 20:9; Isa. 53:6; 64:6; Rom. 3:10-12,23; Gal. 3:22; I Jn. 1:8; 5:19.

43. Matt. 26:39,42,44; John 17:4-5,12; I Cor. 15:22; I Tim. 2:5; L.C. 31,3; Con.F. 7:3-6.

44. Matt. 24:22,31; 25:34; Lk. 13:7; John 6:37-44; 15:16; 17:2,6,9,11-14; Acts 4:28; Rom. 8:28-33; 9:11-26; Eph. 1:4,5,11; II Tim, 2:10; I Pet. 1:2; S.C. 21; L.C. 31.

45. Matt. 26:28; John 14:31; 15:10; Rom. 5:9,19; Phil. 2:8; Heb. 9:14; 10:9; I Pet. 1:18-19; I Jn. 1:7.

46. Isa. 53:9; John 8:46; II Cor. 5:21; Heb. 4:15; 7:26; I Pet. 1:19; 2:22; I Jn. 3:5.

47. Isa. 7:14; 9:6; John 1:14; Rom. 8:3; Gal. 4:4; Phil. 2:7-8; I Tim. 3:16; Heb. 4:15; 9:22; I Pet. 2:22; I Jn. 3:5; S.C. 22; L.C. 37-40.

48. Rom. 5:10-11; I Cor. 15:3; II Cor. 5:18,21; Eph. 2:16; Col. 1:20; Heb. 2:17; I Pet. 3:18.

49. Acts 13:39; Rom. 5:1; 8:30; I Cor. 1:30; 6:11; Gal. 3:24.

50. Acts 13:38-39; Rom. 3:17-19,22-28; 5:1; 8:30,33; Eph. 1:7; 4:32; Col. 1:14; Tit. 3:4-7; I Jn. 2:12; S.C. 33; L.C. 70, 71; Con.F. 13:1-6.

51. John 17:17; Rom. 6:4,6,14,20; 8:4,13; I Cor. 1:30; Eph. 1:4; 5:26; Phil. 3:21; II Thes. 2:13; II Tim. 2:21; Heb. 10:10; 13:12; I Pet. 1:2; S.C. 35, 36; L.C. 75-78; Con.F. 15:1-3.

52. Psl. 78:52; John 6:37; 10:26-29; 15:16; 17:9,11-12.

53. Lev. 5:7; 12:1-8,18; Matt. 8:20; 15:29; Lk. 2:7,24,51; 16:14; 22:63; John 10:20; Acts 8:33; II Cor. 8:9; Phil. 2:7-8.

54. Matt. 27; Mk. 15; Lk. 23; John 19; Phil. 2:8; Heb. 12:2.

55. Lev. 11:45; Eze. 18:31; Joel 2:12; Matt. 3:2; Mk. 1:15; 6:12; Lk. 13:2-3; John 3:15-16; 5:24; 11:25; 16:28; Acts 3:19; 14:15; 16:31; Rom. 9:33; 10:9; I Cor. 1:21; II Cor. 7:1; Heb. 12:14; Jas. 2:17; I Pet. 1:16; II Pet. 3:11.

56. II Ki. 22:19; Job 42:6; Psl. 5:5; 34:18; 51:17; 97:10; Isa. 55:7; 66:2; Eze. 18:21; Lk. 18:13; II Cor. 7:10; Rev. 2:15-16; S.C. 87; L.C. 71; Con.F. 17:1-6.

57. John 3:16; 6:68; 8:24; 10:9; 14:6; Acts 4:12; I Cor. 3:11; S.C. 85, 86; L.C. 72, 73, 153; Con.F. 16:1-3.

58. John 3:3-8,27; 6:65; 15:5; Acts 16:14; Rom. 5:6; 7:18; I Cor. 12:3; II Cor. 3:5; L.C. 182.

59. Lk. 11:13; Acts 2:38.

60. Matt. 2:1; Lk. 1:5; 2:1-2; The Calendar! Josephus Commentary; Secular history.

61. Gen. 3:15; 12:3; 49:10; Deut. 18:15; Gal. 3:7-9; Heb. 11; plus all Old Testament Messianic prophecies too numerous to list.

62. Gen. 4:2-5; Exo. 30:10; Book of Leviticus; Heb. 9:22; 10:1; 11:4.

63. Isa. 53:7; Matt. 26:28; John 1:29,36; I Cor. 5:7; Gal. 1:4; Eph. 5:2; Heb. 10:10; I Pet. 1:19; Rev. 5:6; 6:1; 7:9; 15:3; 21:22.

64. Jer. 10:10; John 18:37; Acts 3:22-23; Heb. 4:15; Rev. 19:16; S.C. 21-23; L.C. 35-36; Con.F. 8:1-8.

65. Same as for Question 64.

66. John 1:4; 14:26; 15:15; S.C. 27; L.C. 43.

67. Heb. 2:17; 4:14-16; 5:5-6; 6:20; 7:26; 8:1; 9:28; 10:1-12; S.C. 25; L.C. 44.

68. II Chron. 20:6; Pro. 20:22; Isa. 9:7; 32:1; 33:22; Jer. 23:5; John 1:49; I Cor. 15:25; I Tim. 6:15; Rev. 1:5; 17:14; 19:16; **S.C.** 26; **L.C.** 45.

69. Job 8:9; Psl. 73:22; Ecc. 8:7; 9:12; 11:5; Rom. 8:26; I Cor. 1:19-21; II Pet. 1:21.

70. Gen. 6:5; Rom. 3:10,12,23; **Cr.Ref.** 35-37.

71. Exo. 14:14; Rom. 7:15; II Cor. 12:9-10.

72. Exo. 20:2-17; 31:18; 32:15-16; 34:1; Deut. 5:7-21; 10:4.

73. Deut. 10:4.

74. Deut. 6:5; Matt. 22:37-38; Mk. 12:29-30.

75. Lev. 19:18; Deut. 10:1-4; Matt. 7:12; 22:39; Mk. 12:31; Rom. 13:9-10; **L.C.** 122.

76. Deut. 6:5; Matt. 22:37-39; Mk. 12:29-31; I Thes. 4:9; **S.C.** 41-44; **L.C.** 98-102.

77. Lk. 10:30-37.

78. Pro. 8:17; John 16:27; Rom. 8:28.

79. Psl. 7:11.

80. Exo. 20:3; Deut. 5:7.

81. Exo. 34:14; Psl. 29:2; Matt. 4:10; **S.C.** 45-48; **L.C.** 103-106; **Con.F.** 23:1.

82. Exo. 20:4-6; 34:14; Deut. 5:8-10.

83. Exo. 34:14; Deut. 4:15-19; Jn. 4:24; I Jn. 5:21; **S.C.** 50-52; **L.C.** 108-110; **Con.F.** 23:1-8.

84. Exo. 20:7; Deut. 5:11.

85. Lev. 19:12; Isa. 6:3; Eze. 36:20-23; 39:7,25; Matt. 6:9; Jas. 5:12; S.C. 54-56; L.C. 112-114.

86. Exo. 20:8-11; Deut. 5:12-15.

87. Lev. 19:30; 23:3; Isa. 58:13-14; S.C. 58,61,62; L.C. 116,118-121; Con.F. 23:8.

88. Acts 20:7; I Cor. 16:2; S.C. 59.

89. John 20:1,19; S.C. 59.

90. Isa. 58:13-14; Matt. 12:12; Lk. 4:16; S.C. 60; L.C. 117.

91. Exo. 20:12; Deut. 5:16.

92. Exo. 21:15,17; Deut. 21:18-23; S.C. 64; L.C. 124-133.

93. Exo. 20:13; Deut. 5:17; Rom. 13:9.

94. Lev. 19:17-18; Matt. 5:21-26,39; 26:52; S.C. 68-69; L.C. 135-136.

95. Exo. 20:14; Deut. 5:18.

96. Matt. 15:19; 19:1-12,18; Lk. 16:18; 18:20; Phil. 4:8; I Thes. 4:3-6; Rom. 12:1; Heb. 13:4;S.C. 71-72; L.C. 138-139.

97. Exo. 20:15; Deut. 5:19; Rom. 13:9.

98. Lev. 19:11,13; Pro. 6:6-11; 13:4; 19:15; 20:4,13; Rom. 12:11; Eph. 4:28; Tit. 2:10; I Pet. 4:15; S.C. 74-75; L.C. 141-142.

99. Exo. 20:16; Deut. 5:20; Rom. 13:9.

100. Lev. 19:11; Pro. 21:6; Eph. 4:25; S.C. 77-78; L.C. 144-145.

101. Exo. 20:17; Deut. 5:21; Rom. 13:9; Gal. 5:26.

102. Job 1:21; Psl. 41:1-2; 49:16-17; 119:36; Pro. 11:24-26; Ecc. 5:10-19; Matt. 13:22; Mk. 7:21; 23; 10:23-25; Lk. 12:15; Rom. 15:1-2; I Cor. 13:4; Phil. 4:11-13; S.C. 80-81; L.C. 147-148.

103. Deut. 27:26; I Ki. 8:46; Gal. 3:10; Jas. 2:10; Cr.Ref. 27,34-36,70.

104. Deut. 27:26; Rom. 3:20; 5:20; 7:7; Gal. 3:24-25; I Tim. 1:9; L.C. 94-97; Con.F. 31:5; Cr.Ref. 35,42.

105. Matt. 21:22; John 15:7; Acts 16:25-26; Phil. 4:6; Jas. 5:16-18; I Jn. 3:22; 5:14-15; S.C. 98; L.C. 178-179; Con.F. 23:3-4.

106. John 14:13-14; 15:16; 16:24; Cr.Ref. 49-50,67,70.

107. Matt. 6:9-13; Lk. 11:2-4; S.C. 99-100; L.C. 186-189.

108. Same as for Question 107.

109. None.

110. Matt. 6:9; Lk. 11:2.

111. Lev. 22:2; Deut. 5:11; 28:58; Isa. 29:23; 57:15; Eze. 36:21-23; Dan. 2:20; Matt. 6:9; Lk. 11:2; S.C. 101; L.C. 190; Cr.Ref. 84-85.

112. Matt. 6:10; Lk. 11:2; Rev. 22:20.

113. Psl. 51:18; Isa. 62:6; Eze. 3:17; Matt. 10:7,27; Mk. 16:15; Lk. 9:2,60; Acts 5:20; 10:36; Rom. 10:1; II Cor. 4:5; Col. 1:28; II Thes. 3:1; I Tim. 1:3-4; 6:2; II Tim. 2:25; 4:2; I Pet. 5:2; S.C. 102; L.C. 191.

114. Matt. 6:10; Lk. 11:2.

115. Psl. 103:20-22; 119:34; Acts 21:14; Rom. 12:2; Eph. 6:6; Heb. 13:21; Jas. 4:25; I Jn. 2:17; **S.C.** 103; **L.C.** 192.

116. Matt. 6:11; Lk. 11:3.

117. Psl. 23:1,5; Pro. 10:22; 30:8; Isa. 41:10; Matt. 6:25-33; 10:29-31; 14:20; Lk. 12:7,22-31; Phil. 4:19; I Tim. 4:4-5; I Pet. 5:7; **S.C.** 104; **L.C.** 193.

118. Matt. 6:12; Lk. 11:4.

119. Psl. 51:1; Matt. 6:12,14-15; Lk. 11:4; Rom. 3:24-25; **S.C.** 105; **L.C.** 194.

120. Matt. 6:13; Lk. 11:4.

121. Psl. 51:10; 19:13; Matt. 26:41; I Cor. 10:13; **S.C.** 106; **L.C.** 195; **Cr.Ref.** 28-30,67,70.

122. I Cor. 11:23-29; **S.C.** 93; **L.C.** 164; **Con.F.** 29:4; 30:1; 31:1-8.

123. Same as for Question 122.

124. Matt. 28:18-20; I Cor. 11:24-26; **L.C.** 164.

125. Matt. 26:26; Mk. 14:22; Lk. 22:19; Rom. 9:8; I Cor. 10:16-17,21; Gal. 3:27,29; 6:15; **S.C.** 91-92; **L.C.** 161-163; **Con.F.** 29:1-3,5.

126. John 3:5; Acts 2:38; 10:48; 22:16; Eph. 5:26; **S.C.** 94; **L.C.** 165; **Con.F.** 30:2-3.

127. Acts 2:38; 10:48; 22:16; Rom. 6:4; I Cor. 6:11; Col. 2:11-12; Tit. 3:5.

128. Matt. 28:19; **Cr.Ref.** 7-8.

129. Josh. 24:15; Mk. 16:16; John 4:53; Acts 2:38-39; 16:15,31-34; I Cor. 7:14; S.C. 95; L.C. 166; Con.F. 30:4,5,7; the book, "Believers and Their Seed" by Herman Hoeksema.

130. Gen. 8:21; Rom. 3:10,12,23; Jas. 2:10; Cr.Ref. 34-38,42,70,104.

131. Matt. 19:13-14; Mk. 10:13-16; Lk. 18:15-16.

132. Rom. 6:4; Gal. 3:26-27; L.C. 167.

133. I Cor. 11:26; S.C. 96; L.C. 168,175-177; Con.F. 31:1-4.

134. I Cor. 11:24; L.C. 169-170; Con.F. 31:5-6.

135. Matt. 26:28; Rom. 11:27; I Cor. 11:25; Heb. 12:24; L.C. 169-170; Con.F. 31:5-6.

136. I Cor. 11:26-34; S.C. 97; L.C. 171-174; Con.F. 31:7-8; Cr.Ref. 55-57, 76-77.

137. Psl. 16:10; Matt. 16:21; 17:23; 20:19; 26:32; 27:63-64; 28:6; Mk. 8:31; 9:9; 14:28; John 2:19; Acts 26:22-23; Heb. 13:20.

138. Isa. 53:12; Lk. 22:32; 23:34; John 14:16; 17:9; Rom. 8:34; Heb. 4:14-16; 7:25; L.C. 55; Con.F. 8:1-8; Cr. Ref. 67,70.

139. Matt. 26:64; Mk. 14:62; Lk. 21:27; Acts 1:11, 17:31; Rom. 2:16; Heb. 9:28; II Pet. 3:10; Rev. 20:12; L.C. 56; Con.F. 35:1-3.

140. Gen. 3:19, 18:27; Psl. 90:5-6; 103:14; Ecc. 12:7; Lk. 23:43; II Cor. 5:8; L.C. 88; Cr.Ref. 17-20.

141. I Thes. 4:16.

142. Pro. 14:12; Matt. 3:12; 18:8-9; 25:41; II Cor. 11:15; Heb. 9:27; Rev. 20:15; 21:8,27; L.C. 89.

143. Matt. 10:28; 13:42; Mk. 9:44; Lk. 16:23; Rev. 14:10-11; 16:10-11; 18:10; 20:10.

144. Num. 23:10; Psl. 116:15; Pro. 14:32; Lk. 16:22; John 14:2-3; Rom. 14:8; I Cor. 6:2; Phil. 1:21; I Thes. 4:17; I Pet. 1:4; Rev. 3:21; 5:10; 21:27; S.C. 38; L.C. 90.

145. John 14:2-3; Acts 7:55-56; II Cor. 5:1; Rev. 7:9,17; 21:1-4,18-25.

Citations to **Shorter Catechism, Larger Catechism, Confession of Faith**, and **Cross References**, abbreviated as **S.C., L.C., Con.F.** and **Cr.Ref.**, include also references to proof texts thereunder.

APPENDIX A
BACKGROUND

We've been asked how to institute a catechism program. Ours grew out of the desire of several of the children to **HAVE BIBLE SCHOOL ALL YEAR LONG.** Not wanting to miss an opportunity to teach the Lord's Word to hungry hearts, we patterned our catechism program after that of Bible school, and continued to hold it one day a week for two hours during the summer, and one hour and fifteen minutes during the school year. Do not try to meet on holidays. It will become more work than fun if children are expected to attend classes on any of their free time, whether for teachers' meetings or whatever. By meeting all year there's more freedom to cancel any time there is an epidemic among the children, too many unavailable teachers, or other unforeseen problems. We found this to be a successful procedure, and prefer not disbanding for the summer months.

The Orthodox Presbyterian Church published **COVENANT CHILDREN'S CATECHUMEN COURSE** which we used as our guide. Dr. Jack Scott, of the Christian Education Committee of the Presbyterian Church in America, did an excellent job of writing in additional study courses to supplement the suggested requirements of each grade level. Rev. Tom Kay, Sr. has published a similar booklet entitled **TRAIN UP A CHILD**, which is patterned after the OPC publication. We are hoping our Christian Education Committee will combine the best of these two, including Dr. Scott's additions, giving us a study course guide which will better suit the needs of this program, and challenge the young people to their fullest potential.

The Catechism program is different from the Sunday School program. In Sunday School the children are taught the Bible content and its application to their lives. Too often all that is required of a Sunday School teacher is to be **WILLING,** since adequate material is furnished from which to make preparation.

The Catechism program is **DOCTRINAL**. The teacher should be thoroughly familiar and in accord with the doctrines of the Presbyterian Church. There is no specific study material to follow. The teacher's aim is to teach theology to children, in **THEIR** language, so that it is understood as well as learned. This is not to say that we do not teach the Bible for the Bible is the basis of all our beliefs. In some churches only the elders are allowed to teach catechism classes. It is excellent to have at least one elder available to teach, provided he knows the church's doctrines, and is interested in helping children understand them. It is good when the pastor is sympathetic to the program and willing to teach also. When he is not, it is better that he be freed from this responsibility, for **ENTHUSIASM** is one of the requirements for a good catechism teacher. To be excited over what you are teaching, and eager to share with the children the wealth of knowledge available, is a mark of a good catechism teacher.

A love for the children is important. Give them the feeling that **YOU LOVE BEING THERE**; it has a good effect on their attitude about attending. When the Bible verses are taught with a sense of amazement at what the Word is saying to us — or church history is taught with awe at what the martyrs suffered without recanting, good discussion and prayer should follow. A teacher who has been coerced into the program will not be excited or enthusiastic, and that attutude will affect the children.

Most churches have teen-agers who will want to **HELP** with the program but not want to participate as learners, or catechumen. It is wise **NOT** to use them as helpers in any capacity unless they are willing to participate as learners. Being allowed to help marks one as older or more responsible, and promotes drop outs, as the older children will begin either to expect to be helpers, or consider themselves too old to continue as learners. The best practice is to require older children helping with the program to participate as catechumen, learning the required memory work along with the others.

A word of caution: Teachers and workers should know how to manage discipline. It is an injustice to the child to be taught (through poor discipline) that he has to respect neither the house of

God nor the Lord's servant. We know there is disagreement regarding the attitude toward the church **BUILDING**, but any place being used for the Lord's work should be treated with reverence. Our observation has been that the children of today are less disciplined and less respectful of their elders than even ten years ago. One of our purposes is to teach them to have a good Christian testimony at all times. Their behaviour at Catechism Program should be above reproach.

One of the most successful programs with which we are acquainted is that of Faith Presbyterian Church in Birmingham. Credit for the success of their catechism program is given to the prayers of the church members. It is important to keep the program before the congregation as a matter of prayer. There should be a definite time for the teachers to have prayer together every week. The best time for this is probably immediately before or after the Catechism session. This is one reason it is good for the teachers not to be responsible for the transportation of any of the children unless, of course, some of their riders are old enough and responsible enough to care for the younger riders during prayer.

Most important, at the very outset, is to have a meeting of all the parents and session members, to explain exactly what you plan to do with the program. The whole-hearted cooperation of parents and officers is essential to a successful program. Serve refreshments, and allow ample time for questions. At this time explain **EVERY FACET** of the program. They should know everything you intend doing during those times you have the children of the church. This will also be a good time to enlist the additional help you will need.

APPENDIX B

WORKERS

TRANSPORTATION:

Ideally there should be a transportation person or committee responsible for picking the children up at the schools and bringing them to the classes. This frees teachers from added responsibility that contributes to haste and anxiety. If a teacher transporting a number of children is unable to come, there's the last-minute job of arranging for those children to be picked up by someone else. It is helpful if the same person bringing them picks them up after class. Everything possible should be done to facilitate and expedite the program.

PLAY LEADERS:

If the children arrive at the church at different times, due to varying school dismissals, have a young man and a young lady there to play outdoors with them until all arrive.

HOSTESS:

If possible, put the refreshments completely into the hands of someone who will be responsible for seeing that they are provided each time. If you have many children in the program, or few workers, it is a big help for the person furnishing the refreshments to serve them, and clean up afterwards.

SONG LEADER:

If you have a singing period, someone is needed to lead who will teach the theology of the hymns and also teach the children to enjoy happy melodious choruses. The children can sing acappella, but a pianist can be a big help. In small churches the singing time can also double as a junior choir rehearsal, allowing the children to sing periodically in the church services.

TEACHERS:

The program can be begun with only two teachers. As the children progress in the memorization work, or more attend, a teacher can be added for every age level.

HEARERS:

It is very helpful to have one or more hearers. They will hear memory work on an individual basis during group participation in other sessions. As each child recites memory work to the hearer, the hearer will then give the child an assignment slip filled in with the required memory work to be working on during the next week, to be recited the following class period. It is also a great incentive if the hearer will give the child an M & M for each Bible verse, catechism answer, or hymn verse passed off.

HELPERS:

One or more helpers are also a great help to the program. The helper takes an individual aside for the entire class period and helps him memorize in order to catch up with his age group. They work with slow learners and children whose parents are not helping them memorize at home. Sometimes a helper can handle several children together if they are all working on the same passage or catechism answer.

DIRECTOR:

The program will run more smoothly if one person is in charge of the entire program. This person will be available to handle disciplinary problems when the teachers need assistance. The director will also be available to substitute for any absent teacher.

The director would be responsible for getting all announcements regarding the program into the church bulletin; writing letters to parents when needed; mailing cards to absentee participants; keeping assignment slips mimeographed, game equipment in order, parties and play days anticipated and planned (with the help of the other workers) and anything else that fails to come under any particular worker's job.

Don't let this impressive list of workers discourage you. The program can be carried on very effectively with two, three, or four workers. This will be explained later.

APPENDIX C

MECHANICS

During school months, one hour and fifteen minutes should be sufficient for Catechism each week. This allows for:

1. play time	15 minutes
2. refreshments	15 minutes
3. singing	15 minutes
4. classes	30 minutes

During summer months, the time can be extended to two hours one morning a week, to be divided as follows:

1. play time	30 minutes
2. refreshments	15 minutes
3. singing	30 minutes
4. classes	45 minutes

PLAY TIME:

Some have found that outdoor recreation before session begins is a good way to work off some of the energy built up during school hours. Others find that a little play only increases the restless spirit. If you have fifteen minutes of play time after school prior to the sessions, try using it for regular secular play some of the time, and for supportive games the other times. Or use the time exclusively for supportive games, which are a valuable aid to the learning process. The young man and young lady helping can work with the children, teaching them courtesy and Christian attitudes. This means correcting them when they insist on being first at bat, or first in anything. During play time we try constantly to remind them of two principles: 1. They are to play and act as they think Jesus would. 2. They are to treat the other fellow as though he were Jesus. Remind them of this consistently, that they may learn how to play as Christians. If you extend the play time to thirty minutes in the summer, try using half for active secular play, and half for supportive games, which will be explained later. Use common sense and the knowledge of your own group in setting your schedule. Having fifteen minutes of secular activity each time, then one whole day occasionally (once a month, once a quarter, on rainy days, as rewards for extra hard work, etc.) in which there are no classes, just refreshments and supportive games, have proven highly effective.

Boys usually like to play whatever ball game is in season, and the girls like to jump rope. If the grounds are conducive, hide-and-seek, red rover, or some other active game for the whole group is good.

When playing two sides against each other, never appoint captains to choose team-mates. The same children unpopular at school will be chosen last at Catechism. Our purpose is to teach children to treat each other fairly, each esteeming others as better than themselves. Instead, quickly divide the group into boys against girls, or the odd grades against the even grades, or blondes against brunettes, etc. Do not let any child get by with belittling or ridiculing another player's inability or faulty play. Use this time to teach the golden rule **APPLIED** in daily life.

Boys will generally play more readily than girls. You will have girls who want to watch instead of participate sometimes. Encourage, insist, that they all play. This is a good time to help children who feel insecure or inferior, as well as those with attitudes of superiority. Learning to play together in a Christian context is important, and this may well be the only time this concept is taught the children in practice as well as theory.

REFRESHMENTS:

We are eating at church meetings so often today, we may be teaching our children that we pay, reward, or bribe people to come to church functions. We're in danger of giving the impression that the church program itself is not sufficient to feed us without physical food. We suggest that refreshments be kept very simple and preferably varied. If someone brings cookies, let the children drink water. If they're served Kool-aid, they do not need a cookie with it. Someone may bring a large bowl of popcorn, a basket of fresh roasted peanuts, an apple or banana or tangerine per child, peanut butter crackers, popsicles, ice cream cups, hot chocolate, coca-cola, cup cakes, popcorn balls, candy bar, etc. A little imagination and loving preparation on the part of someone will make catechism time fun. This responsibility should not be on the teachers.

Insist that the boys allow the girls to be served first. Read and explain I Peter 3:7. Help both sexes to understand that girls are the weaker vessels in God's economy, because **HE** made us that way. The boys can learn good manners and politeness and courtesy in catechism class, because often they're not being taught at home. The boys should be taught to open car doors for ladies, including mothers and sisters, to offer to help ladies up and down church steps, etc. It's important also to teach them the reason. These manners are based on Scripture, so we're teaching them the practical application of Scripture. When a girl comes into class the boys should rise and offer their chairs, as gentlemen, or bring in another if needed. Some parents will buck this teaching, calling it silly or premature, so you have the job of teaching God's Word often **WITHOUT** any help from the parents! In teaching the boys to allow the girls to be first in line, you must work with the manners of the girls also. They are not to **INSIST** on being first! As Christians we do not demand our rights; we forego them when the other person is inconsiderate. We are gracious and thankful when we **ARE** treated as ladies. The girls must learn the meek and quiet spirit of I Peter 3:4.

Instead of allowing the children to say "I don't like that" or "I'm allergic to this," teach them to say a gracious "No, thank you." They must be taught to thank whoever serves the refreshments. Teach them not to ask for second helpings, or to take two the first time around. Christian courtesy requires respect for the other person's needs and rights and desires over your own. If there are second servings, they can be offered by the hostess, not requested by the guest. These suggestions sound foolish to some teachers and young mothers. We are to teach the children Christian principles in **EVERY AREA** of life. If you haven't previously worked with children, you are probably in for a surprise at the lack of good manners on the part of children today, even from Christian homes!

They are also to thank the Lord for the food. Get different ones of the children to ask the blessing at refreshment time each week. If they are reluctant to volunteer, talk to them about Christ's denying anyone before the Father who is reluctant to acknowledge his relationship with Christ before people. We should never feel hesitant to talk to our Lord and our Redeemer. If we know Him and love Him, then as His child we like to talk to Him just as we do with an earthly father. Be consistent in this training also, for at **ALL TIMES** in Catechism sessions we are teaching Christian conduct.

One requirement of the program is a complete reading of the **CHILD'S STORY BIBLE**, by Catherine Vos. Ideally there should be a copy of this book in every home to be used in family devotions. Since there isn't, and because many parents do not read to their children or have family altar, we read one story from this book at each refreshment period. This keeps the children quieter than if left free to play while eating. They sit on the floor of the church kitchen while the story is read to them, and they discuss it and have a question period.

Refreshment time should not take over fifteen minutes. At the end of that time, if one child wants to hold on to his cup or finish his food, you merely take it gently, telling him that refreshment time is over. One or two of these experiences will teach the children not to dawdle over their food or play with it. This prevents waiting for them to finish, upsetting the entire schedule.

SINGING

During singing period, I suggest teaching them happy melodious choruses similar to those often used in Bible School. They are fun to sing, and song time can be a very happy time. Many scriptures have been put to music. Rev. Ford Williams, P. O. Box

794, Mississippi State, Miss. 39762 has a good collection of these. Teach the children to associate the correct chorus with the Scripture reference! Any money donated to the program could well be spent on Child Evangelism visual aid songs. Many songs can be put into signs or book form or other ideas you'll conceive as you work with them over a period of time. Making some of these songs is a good project for your P.Y.F. Include in the music time hymns being learned by the various age-levels. Also include the Doxology and Gloria Patri occasionally, and the hymn-of-the-month if your church has one. This helps them with their memory work. Some good hymns with sound theology should be included each week. In all of these songs, take opportunity to discuss what the words are saying. **CRUSADE HYMN STORIES** by Cliff Barrows, or some other good book on hymnody should be available to the song leader.

As the program begins to move smoothly from one part to another, fifteen minutes for music should be ample, with thirty minutes during the summer.

If one or more of the children do not sing, talk to them about the **OBLIGATION** of Christians to sing! Remind them of the **REQUIREMENT** in Psalms to sing unto the Lord, which never mentions whether you have a good voice or whether you **LIKE** to sing. Children should be taught that singing is an act of obedience unto the Lord, not an elective. Encourage each one to participate to the Lord's glory. Many times they can be gently prodded with loving teasing, provided it is not caustic.

APPENDIX D

CLASSES

After singing, go to classes. The teacher should open the class with prayer. I suggest this for this reason: Some child has prayed at refreshment time. We want to teach them to approach our Heavenly Father without hesitation or embarrassment. Children's prayers can be beautifully sincere. However, many times they can be rote. Do not let the children do all the praying. If a child asks the blessing, the teachers may open the classes with prayer. if an adult asks the blessing, it will maintain good balance to allow a child to open the class time with prayer. This is a time to settle down to serious study. The tone of the classroom can be set with the opening prayer.

One way to handle memory work is to ask at the beginning of the class period how many have memory work ready to recite. When they raise their hands, tell one to go to the hearer, and when he returns, the next one designated can slip out, and when he returns, the next, etc. Thus each one knows when he is quietly to leave the room to recite memory work to the hearer, and who has his book (**Covenant Children's Catechumen Course**, or **Train Up a Child**, as explained earlier), and who will record in it the memory work accomplished each week. This method allows them to slip quietly out to the hearer in the order given, without disturbing the lesson period.

At this time the hearer fills out an assignment slip to give to the child. A stencil with something similar to the following typed out on it four or five times, run off periodically and cut into individual slips will keep the necessary supply available:

NAME _____

Memory work assignment for (date)_____

> Learn catechism answers word for word as written in Catechism for Young Children. Repeat Scripture reference before and after reciting Scripture passage. All memory work must be quoted perfectly without error or prompting. Memorize from King James, New American Standard, or New International Version only.

Try to learn: _____

_____

_____

(Thank you, Parents, for helping)

If you are limited as to the number of workers, try this procedure: While one worker is serving the refreshments, reading the story, and leading the singing, the other can be hearing memory work, dispensing M & Ms and making out assignment slips. (I have been agreeably surprised at how well the children keep up with their slips. One or two consistently misplace theirs. I consider them important enough to be delivered or mailed to the children who leave them.) Any child who did not get to recite his memory work can do so at the beginning of the class period. Two workers can divide the group, one teaching the more advanced group, the other teaching the lower level group, or younger children. If this division puts too many children in one class, allow the children heard first to act then as hearers assisting the teacher with the rest of the group. This is helpful to the teacher, fun to the students, and is an incentive to memorize, as only those who have recited may serve as hearers. Follow class period and close the program with fifteen minutes of supportive games in place of the first fifteen minutes of play.

One of the best incentives for memory work, as explained earlier, is to keep a bowl of M & Ms on the table.

At the meeting for parents, teachers and session prior to establishing your program, explain that your purpose in the program will not be to teach the memory work to the children. That will be the parent's job. The Catechism program is established in order to help the children **UNDERSTAND** what they are reciting. For this reason, a Bible with cross references, a good concordance, some sound commentaries and books on systematic theology will be your study material. The tremendous value of this program lies in the fact that we are teaching doctrine to children. It will be the job of the teachers to explain the Bible verses and catechism answers so that the children can understand what they are reciting. That is why it is necessary for the teacher to understand first before he or she can teach the theology to the children.

HELPERS:

Use all the mnemonics about which you can learn. Write the verse or catechism answer on the board, have the child or children, if working with more than one, read it aloud over and over. Each time it is read, erase another word at random until finally the whole verse is erased and it is still being repeated. This encourages the children very much to see how easy it is to memorize a verse. Always remember to write the reference before and after the verse.

Another method is to pair off the children who are working on the same verse or question, and let one teach the other until that one can say it without error, then reverse the process. They always love being the teacher.

Let the child or children be your teacher, and you memorize the verse. Work at really memorizing it, going over and over it as the child prompts you, until you've learned it well. (If you're as old as I am, believe me, this won't be easy!) Then you help the child learn it.

Have them say one phrase of the verse five times aloud. Then have them repeat the next phrase five times, then put the two phrases together and repeat five times. Then say another phrase, add it to the two first phrases, then another, etc. Keep on until they can repeat the entire verse five times.

Explain the verse thoroughly, drawing out discussion and questions so they fully understand the personal application. Then have them read it aloud and explain it to you until they have memorized it and can quote it.

If teaching several, go around the room, letting each child supply the next word of the verse or answer until the whole is completed. Allow them to prompt and help each other until all have learned it and each can say it individually.

Go around the room, letting each child read it aloud, then repeat a second time, letting each say as much as he can from memory and reading the rest, until each child can quote the passage without looking.

Encourage them to think of mnemonics that will help them learn.

APPENDIX E

SUPPORTIVE GAMES

These are games adapted from secular games. Most of them have been built around the memorization program, but all are Bible based. Many games lend themselves to Bible adaptation. You will think of others as you play these with the children.

Although in some of the games you will gear your questions to the memorization level of the child, in some of the games each child is responsible for knowing the whole catechism.

The whole group can play some of these games together well, and should whenever possible. Closely graded age divisions in our culture have resulted in children's not being compatible with anyone not their own age. These games are a good means of teaching the compatibility of varying age groups. However, many of the games cannot be played by younger children. The natural division seems to come between the third and fourth grades.

Do not offer prizes. And there is no reason to give excessive importance to winning. The competitive instinct provides enough incentive for the children to enjoy winning, without any additional reward being necessary. Teach them to be good winners and good losers.

WHO AM I?

This game can be purchased at some Christian book stores. Your Presbyterian Youth Fellowship or some member of the congregation can make yours.

Equipment: A set of cards, each with the name of a Bible character and four hints as to his identity.

Directions: Divide the group into two sides. Taking one card, call out the first hint to the character's identity. Wait briefly. If no one knows who it is, read the second hint. The first person to identify the character calls out the name. If correct, his side will receive the card. If he is incorrect, one card will be taken from his side. At the end of the game, when all the cards have been used, the side with the most cards wins. If neither side knew the answer after all four hints were read, tell them who it is, and put that card aside.

REFRESHMENT LINE UP
Equipment: A felt-tipped pen, some 3 x 5 cards, straight pins, a whistle.

Directions: Write the names of some of the books of the Old Testament on the cards, one book to each card. Do not use books in consecutive order, unless you have thirty-nine children present! Pin a card to the front of each child. Blow a whistle when it is time to start, and see how long it takes them to line up in the correct order!

SELF-IDENTIFICATION
Equipment: A felt-tipped pen, some 3 x 5 cards, straight pins.

Directions: Write the name of a Bible character on each card. Pin one card to the back of each child. Do not tell the child who he is. The object of the game is to see who can discover his own identity first. He does this by asking the other children questions about himself. They answer as briefly as possible. Or they can give him one fact about himself. Each one gives rather veiled answers, although truthful, for each wants to find out his own identity before the one whose questions he is answering! Small children cannot play this game well. It is better for older children.

DODGE BALL
Equipment: A big open space, and a soft large plastic ball.

Directions: Draw an imaginary large circle, putting all the children into it and all the workers around the perimeter. One worker throws the ball, trying to hit one or more of the children, who dodge, staying within the circle. If a child is hit, the worker throwing the ball calls out a catechism question or required Bible verse, then counts to ten. If the child starts giving the correct answer before the worker arrives at ten, he gets to stay within the circle. If not, he has to get out of the game. If there are a limited number of workers, the child thrown out may help throw the ball.

The last child to stay in the circle wins the game. A variation of this is to call out letters of the alphabet instead of catechism questions, expecting the child to recite a Bible verse that starts with that letter.

MUSICAL SACK

Equipment: A paper sack containing a number of catechism questions and Bible verses typed out on individual slips of paper. It is nice to have a piano and pianist, or whistle, but with a small group neither of these is necessary.

Directions: Have the group form a circle. They are to pass the sack around until the music stops, the whistle blows, or you clap your hands. At the given signal, the one holding the sack must draw out a slip and quote the proper memory work. If done correctly he may stay in the circle. If not, he has to drop out.

SPOON

Equipment: A number of spoons, preferably plastic. A set of cards on which are written all the books of the New Testament, in sets of four — that is, four II Peters, four Marks, etc. These are available at Christian book stores. If not, make up a set from 4 x 6 index cards cut in half, with the names of the books written vertically in two corners with a felt-tipped pen, similar to bridge cards.

```
II                          S
C                           N
O                           A
R                           I
I                           H
N                           T
T                           N
H                           I
I                           R
A                           O
N                           C
S                           II
```

Directions: Seat the children in a circle. Put a pile of spoons in the center of the circle, one less spoon than the number of children participating. Deal the cards until all are gone. The fact that some children may have received one more than others makes no difference. If there are too few children playing to be able to handle the whole set, take out several books of cards, giving each child about seven or eight cards. The object of the game is to acquire a book or set of all four of one New Testament Book title. They cannot make a book from one John, two II John, and one III John! When you clap your hands, the children are to pass a discarded card, face down, to the person to their left, and pick up the card that has been placed before them. Clap your hands again after they've had time to rearrange their hands, allowing them to pass a discard again. Continue this until one child has a book. He shows that he has a book or set of four by taking a spoon from the pile. At that signal, all the children dive for a spoon, because the child who fails to get a spoon will get a "J" by his name on the score board. Make the one who completed the set show it to you, to be sure he has four of the same book. If he does not, he gets a "J" by his name. Shuffle, deal, and play again. The first child to get J-U-D-A-S spelled out beside his name is subject to some ridiculous stunt the children require, or merely loses the game.

Note: Generally, children in the first three grades can't play this game well with older children. The pressure is so great they ruin the game by reaching out for a spoon before they have completed a book.

TIC-TAC-TOE

Equipment: A Bible tic-tac-toe game from a Christian book store. If not available, simply have several large sheets of paper or poster board on hand, and a felt-tipped pen. Large pads of paper for such purposes are available from school supply houses.

Directions: Draw a large square divided into nine equal squares. Divide the group into two teams. Ask one team a catechism question. If they answer correctly, place an X in whichever square they choose. Ask the other team a question or Bible reference. Place an O in the square they choose if answered correctly. Keep this up until one side wins.

Variation: Pre-draw the squares, and write into each square a catechism question or Bible reference, then let the children choose the block they want to answer. Draw several ahead to have ready.

DARTS, MARBLE THROW, BOWLING etc. Most of the games listed under PARTIES, "Carnival", can be used as supportive games, requiring very little equipment, which can be used over and over again.

BIBLE BASEBALL

Equipment: A note pad or poster board for a score board, a chair for you and one for the score keeper by you, a catechism book, and a study guide with all the memorization requirements in it.

Directions: Divide the children into two teams. The first child at bat asks for a single, two-bagger, three-bagger, or home run. This means an easy question, semi-easy, semi-hard, or hard. Govern your questions accordingly. If he answers the question, he stands at the appropriate spot on the imaginary miniature field before you. Chairs can be placed at each base if they prefer to sit, with your chair marking home plate. If he misses, he is out. One or two outs for each side, rather than three, gives the other team a quicker turn at bat, making the game move faster. No bases are stolen. A child does not move from his base until pushed off by the next player.

HANGMAN

This is a good game to play on rainy days.

Equipment: A chalk board, chalk and eraser, or large poster board and felt-tipped pen.

Directions: Divide the group into two teams. If you have a small group, instead of dividing them, each child can have a turn at guessing. Draw a blank on the board for each letter of the word you have chosen from the Bible. Now ask the first child to guess one of the letters in the word. If he guesses correctly, write the letter above the blank in its proper place in the word. If the same letter appears more than once in the word, you only have to write

in one. That means that another child can guess the very same letter
if he wishes. If he guesses a letter that is **NOT** in the word, you
draw one section of the gallows on which to hang him. Continue to
give the children (or teams) turns
until someone has guessed what
the word is (in which case he gets
to write the next blanks on the
board); or the completed gallows
and hanged man are drawn on
the board. It takes eleven misses
to hang the man shown at right.

A _ R A _ _ M

LEMONADE

This is an **OLD** one. No equipment is necessary, except a
fairly large space, with a sidewalk dividing it into two sides.

Directions: Divide the group into two sides, positioning them
on opposite sides of a walk or dividing line. Allow them to go into
huddles to decide what Bible story their team is going to act out.
The first team to decide upon a story and which characters are to
perform (try to use all the team in each pantomime) come to the
edge of the walk, announce their readiness to perform, call out the
first letters of the incident they are depicting, and proceed to act it
out. The other team lines up on the opposite side of the walk
immediately to watch and try to guess what the first team is doing.
The old rhyme went like this:

(1st team)	Bum, bum, bum, here we come.
(2nd team)	What's your trade?
(1st team)	Lemonade!
(2nd team)	How do you make it?
(1st team)	Stir it and shake it.
(2nd team)	What are the initials?
(1st team)	(They announce the initials.)
(2nd team)	Go to work and work all day!

This is the signal to begin. The smaller children like this. The older ones prefer to leave it off.

When the second team guesses what the first team is acting, they call it out and race across the walk or line, capturing as many players from the first team as possible and bringing them back to their side. Of course as soon as the second team calls out the correct answer, the first team runs for their safety spot a safe distance away from the walk.

They originate some clever ideas, once they've learned the game. You may have to help them at first. Example: The initials are S P B F. Have some of the children sit on the ground, watching the whole thing with utter amazement. Have others walking back and forth carrying something, and all dumping their loads in the same spot. One child carries his load, but when dumping it, looks at his arm with amazement, then violently shakes his arm, watches the thing fall, and stomps on it. Those watching from their seat on the ground show shock, then reverence and respect. The second team guesses the answer: Shipwrecked Paul Building a Fire.

SPELL DOWN

All ages. No equipment. Good for indoors.

Directions: Divide the group into two teams, or three if there is a large crowd. Ask the first child a catechism question. If he answers it, he remains standing. If he misses, he sits down. Ask the first child on the next team another, alternating between the teams. The team to have the last child standing wins.

CHARADES

Older children play this better than younger ones.

Equipment: A supply of slips of paper with titles of Bible stories.

Directions: Divide into two teams. Appoint one child from each team or allow each team to choose their own actor. Give one actor a slip of paper. Example: "Joshua marching around Jericho" or "Jesus talking to the woman at the well." The player is to try to act out the whole title, or various words from the title, until his team has figured out what he is acting. Keep record of the number of minutes it takes his team to figure the answer. Then give a slip of paper to the actor from the other team, and keep a record of his time. The fastest side wins.

TWENTY QUESTIONS

This can be played indoors, by older children. No equipment.

Directions: One child thinks of a person, place or object from the Bible. The rest of the group take turns asking him questions about it, which can only be answered with "yes" or "no". They must try to figure out what he has in mind with twenty questions or less. The child who guesses the answer is the one who has the next turn. If you play this long enough, however, you may appoint the child to have the next turn, as some children will guess the answers more than once. Example: (Balaam's mule) Is it in the Old Testament? Is it a person? Is it a place? Was it made of metal? Is it in the Pentateuch? Is it an animal?

PASSWORD

This is an indoor game for older children.

No equipment, except a list of appropriate words from the Scriptures.

Directions: While the rest of the group watch, have two children play at a time. One is given the word from Scripture. His object is to see how fast he can make the other person guess what the word is, by giving him synonyms or related single words. Example: The word is ESTHER. Hints, fired as rapidly as possible, would include woman, queen, Jew, Mordecai, Haman, etc. After this team finishes, try another team with another word. The competition lies in which team can finish in the shortest length of time.

APPENDIX F

PROGRAM FOR THE YEAR

The program should be varied throughout the year, to keep it interesting to the children. Keep it flexible. A suggested schedule for the year is as follows:

Start the first week of school, in August or September. Set for your goal at least one award for every child in the program by Easter. If you have access to the written-in study courses Dr. Jack Scott added to the curriculum, you will note that some age levels cannot be passed until the children have had a course taught them in church creeds, church government, church history, Christian doctine, evangelism, or missions. Your minister should be able to suggest good study courses until the new study guide by the Presbyterian Church in America Christian Education Committee comes out. Plan your classes around these courses in addition to the catechism and Bible passages. When you're teaching the catechism, the emphasis will be on the memorization of the answers. When you're teaching a study course, there can be a let-up from the urgency to complete so much memory work each week. Plan to have each child complete one grade-level by Easter if he is behind his own age level. For those who are up to their own age level, you will want to use the year going into a very thorough teaching of the Bible references, the catechism questions, and the study courses.

When beginning a catechism program, all the children can start in one class, regardless of age. If, however, you have too large a group for this, divide the younger from the older ones. The older ones will memorize faster and complete whole age-levels faster, and will be moved into another class sooner.

The catechism program is practically the only place outside the family where children of varying ages are expected to work and play together. You will be delighted to see their ability to adapt to this interacting. The older children will help little ones find and read songs; the older will help the younger and encourage them in

games, and so on. Remind them that there are no age levels in
Heaven — that all of us will be together there, and this is a good
time to practice getting along with other ages!

After Christmas holidays, when school opens in January,
begin with a new program. Dispense with all teaching in the
classes, and use the class time from January until Easter in a
concentrated all-out effort to pass enough memory work for
EVERY CHILD to receive an award by Easter.

From January to Easter set an **URGENT** atmosphere in your
classes. When the children arrive at Catechism, greet them with an
excited and expectant question as to how much memory work
they're ready to pass. Brag if they have **ANY** to recite. Let them
know how sincerely you're backing them and expecting them to
receive an award. We want them all to reach their own grade level
as soon as possible.

During these months, the children who have reached their age
level can continue memorization of the **Children's** or **Shorter
Catechism**, but concentrate their efforts on helping the others pass
at least one level in order to receive an award. There are two goals:
1. To see that each child receives at least one award each year. 2. To
help the children reach their age level as soon as possible. This
means that in the early years of the program some children will
receive several awards each year — an award for each age level
completed.

During class time, the workers (including the children who are
now helpers during this period) divide the children so that all who
are memorizing the same reference can work together and there
will be plenty of individual help. One young worker may take one
child apart and work with him until he has thoroughly learned the
work that is necessary for him to recite. (If a child **LEARNS** the
work one week, he does not get credit for reciting it until the
NEXT week.) Use all supportive games during this time, in order
to help them as much as possible. As children pass memory work
and approach their goals, the excitement should mount. You might
keep a poster board of the names with stars or checks by the names
for each level passed, but be careful: This **MUST** work as an
incentive for the whole group to help the slow ones, rather than be

cause for pride in others. If you're having a party for them after Easter to honor or reward them for their hard work, they should realize that they are a team, and the whole team has to pass the requirements in order for the whole team to get to have the party.

During these months of feverish effort to memorize the necessary requirements, use all the mnemonics listed under **CLASSES**, Helpers.

Awards can be given twice a year, at Easter and in September, until some of the children reach their own age level (everyone starts in the three year old level) then the awards can be given once a year, at Easter or near the end of school.

A good compensation for them afterwards would be to take the whole group **DURING THE NORMAL CATECHISM PROGRAM** to a good Walt Disney film, to play miniature golf, to a water slide, a skating rink, an ice cream parlor, or some similar entertainment.

The first catechism period after Easter could be used for a party or entertainment suggested. Then embark upon a new program. Start with a different study course, or begin with the catechism and Bible verse teaching and explanations again, or whatever comes next in the study manual. Keep this up until school is out. The last week of school is a good time to use the catechism time again to take them to one of the entertainments suggested. These "fun" times contribute to keeping them interested in the catechism program.

Unless it is necessary for them to know about these surprises ahead of time for a specific reason (as arriving home later than usual, or bringing a swim suit) I suggest you do not tell them ahead whether they are going to have regular class or whether you're taking them for a "treat." This prevents any coming just for the fun, and it rewards those who are faithful in regular attendance. I do not think it is necessary to encourage them to invite a friend. The parties and treats are designed to encourage the children who are faithful in the work of the program, and to teach them to mix well with the whole age spectrum. They are a Christian family, in a sense. And just as the church members should learn to get along in the body of Christ, so should the children, and this is a good place to learn.

The week before school dismisses for Thanksgiving and Christmas, use the catechism time to take the children to a nursing home or some place where they can do something for other people. When taken to a nursing home, remind them to **TOUCH** the older people. These elderly patients get to pat, hug, and love children so very seldom, that they are hungry for love from young people. It is a real blessing to the children to be in a program that expects them to "give out" as well as "take in." As the program progresses, these trips on a more regular basis are excellent for the children.

Curtail catechism classes when the church is having Bible School. Usually there are about six weeks in the summer that can be used for catechism classes. If this works satisfactorily for your group, I'd encourage you to utilize that time. If not, curtail the program through the whole summer. The month of Bible School, or the month before school starts will be a good time for a vacation from the program.

Please keep the program fun, interesting, educational and edifying!

APPENDIX G

AWARDS

The awards given for passing a grade-level can be very inexpensive. These can be pencils, book marks, rulers, balloons, key chains, lapel pins, and other similar objects with Christian emblems or Scriptures on them. If you have access to a Christian book store, you should find plenty of ideas there.

Child Evangelism has a good supply of awards that I like very much. They include bracelets, necklaces, pins, watch fobs, pens, pencils, key rings, and many more such items. All have the five colors of the wordless book on them: The black, representing sin; red, representing the precious blood of Christ; white, representing the heart washed white as snow in the blood; gold, for the streets of Heaven, the Christian's home; and green, for the spiritual growth required of the Christian. These awards give the children many opportunities to tell the plan of salvation to friends and acquaintances, and to share the gospel even with strangers.

As the children progress to higher levels of learning and the work gets harder, more expensive awards may be chosen. The **JUNGLE DOCTOR** books by Paul White, the **SUGAR CREEK GANG**, and the **DANNY ORLIS** series are all good. All the awards should be of a Christian nature.

The church should give a much nicer award for the completion of the child's catechism. Most churches give Bibles or **HALLEY'S HANDBOOK**. They should also be given an appropriate award by the church for completion of the **Shorter Catechism**.

APPENDIX H

PARTIES

Since this is a doctrinal program, requiring work and concentration from the children, I **STRONGLY** recommend a **GOOD** party for them about twice a year. These parties should be well-planned. Here are some suggestions:

Have the Women in the Church sponsor a party for the catechism children, with lavish refreshments and beautiful decorations. I have seen the tables decorated with Bible scenes depicted in paper mache or clay figures, the fellowship hall festooned with balloons and streamers, and the entrance to the fellowship hall lighted with lawn torches or candles and streamers. The children were allowed to plan the games for the occasion, and taught some of their supportive games to the congregation. The awards were given at this time, making it a very memorable occasion honoring the children who had worked so hard.

CARNIVAL

The children can plan a carnival, and invite the whole congregation as their guests. With the help of parents or workers, the children can plan, provide and serve the refreshments. They can make all preparations, including any decorating. In each Sunday school room, put a person, preferably of college age or a catechism teacher. As people arrive, give each one a ribbon of one of two colors, thus dividing the entire group into two teams— the blues and reds, or greens and yellows. As they arrive, send them on their way to the various class rooms to compete in games that will contribute points to their team. The barker in each room will have the blackboard or a poster board lined down the middle. As each participant makes a score for his side, it is registered on the appropriate side of the board. In one room, have a divider that held twenty eggs. In the bottom of each egg division should be pasted a catechism question or a Bible verse that was required memory work in the catechism program. Give each participant three marbles. If he is able to recite the passage or catechism answer pasted in the space into which his marble falls, he gets one point for his team and another throw. The same for marble number two. Three marbles are his limit. If, however, he is unable to answer the first or second question, he does not get to throw his next marble. He does not get points for his team for landing the marble in the container—only if he can answer the question where his marble fell.

In another room have a board with twelve dowels fastened upright onto it, about four inches high. Write the name of an apostle on each post. Give each participant three canning jar rings. If, when tossing a ring, he loops it over a post, he gets one point for his team for each fact he can tell about that particular apostle. If he can tell NONE, of course he does not get to throw his next rings.

In another room, line up ten pasteboard tubes from paper towels, or toilet tissue. Cut them to about six inches in height. Write a catechism question or Bble reference on each one. Line them up straight across, not in the ordinary bowling triangle, and spaced so that only one tube can be hit at a time, and the ball can roll between two without hitting either. Use old tennis balls for bowling. Give each participant two balls. If he can answer the question of the pin knocked down, he gets to throw his second ball, and scores a point for his team.

In another room, make a dart board, sectioned off with catechism questions and Bible verses on it. Give each participant three darts. The same procedure follows to win points for his team.

Other booths can be made by using a pistol that shoots rubber darts, and a board of questions and verses. Or put the minister or youth director or some college student in one long room behind a sheet or board with only his head sticking through. If the participant can hit him with a water-filled balloon, and can answer the question asked from the catechism or recite the Scripture passage called out, he gets one point for his team, but no second throw!

Copy ideas from other sources and adapt them to your carnival. It will be a big success. At the end of the specified time,

when each member of the congregation has raced from one room
to another, piling up points for his team, all gather in the fellowship
hall to sing from a mimeographed sheet songs that the children use
in the catechism program. During this time the *barkers* tally the
points, and at the end of the singing period the winning team is
announced. Lolly-pops can then be passed to each member of the
winning team. Serve delicious refreshments, and go home from a
fun and learning good time.

Variation: instead of each person participating, an adult can
be teamed up with a catechism student, and the adult can do the
throwing and the child the answering.

TREASURE HUNT

Divide the children into teams of equal number to go in cars,
pickups, or station wagons. Give each group a Bible of the same
version from which the clues were taken, and a copy of the first
clue. Each clue should be such that they have to look up Bible
references to know where to go for the next clue. Here are some
examples:

1. Go to the home of a person mentioned in Titus 1:5, whose
last name starts with the same letter as that of the Bible character in
I Kings 3:5. In the yard you will find something mentioned in Psalm
1:3. On this the next clue will be found attached with the
instrument used in Judges 4:21.(answer: a nail in a tree in Elder
Smith's yard)

2. There are several places in our town of which the seventh
word in Romans 6:23 may make you think. If you need further
help, it is also mentioned in the twenty-fifth and twenty-sixth
verses of John 11, and also in the Apostles' Creed. Go there, and the
next clue is on what is mentioned in Matthew 7:13. (the gate of the
cemetery)

3. The fifth and sixth words of Matthew 19:14 combined with
the first word of II Timothy 2:15 should send you to a building in
town. Need another hint? The reason for going there is found in the
answer to catechism question "Why do you need Christ as a

prophet?" The next clue is on what Christ called himself in John 10:7. (door of the elementary school)

4. Go to the **PLACE** mentioned in Psalm 90:1 occupied by the person mentioned in fifteenth word of Mark 10:45. There you will find what the man that walketh not in the counsel of the ungodly in Psalm 1 is likened to. The clue will be tied to something mentioned six times in John 15:1-11. (branch of tree at the manse)

5. This one's easy. Go to the thing in Genesis 28:12, at a combination of John 3:23 and Genesis 11:4 Can't figure it out? It compares to the place of meeting between Jesus and the woman in John 4:6-7. (on the ladder to the water tower)

6. Can you name the books of the New Testament? They're required memory work for the second grade level. One man's name appears four times. In his yard, look for the next clue in what the foolish man built his house upon. (sand pile at John's house)

7. Go to the receptacle for the object named in Galatians 6:11, at the home of what is mentioned in I Timothy 3:10, where live (for the number, John 4:18) (for the object, Genesis 30:1). There you'll find your next clue. (in mail box of a deacon with 5 children)

At each place there should be as many clues as there are teams in cars, so each team can take a clue. Otherwise, the groups will have to leave the one clue where they find it, for the other teams to find also. Other suggestions for clues are: rocks, houses, water, names of people in the congregation, windows, lakes, compass points, songs, numbers.

The last clue can lead the crowd to a box of weiners, buns, mustard, potato chips, drinks, etc. carefully hidden in an appropriate spot for the weiner roast which will be held at the end of the hunt. If you wish, you can end the party by letting each child throw a pine cone into the camp fire after having consumed the refreshments, and tell a testimony to the Lord's goodness, or something they've learned that has helped in everyday situations. Always close with prayer.

A SCAVENGER HUNT

Divide the group into teams, sending them out in pickups or

station wagons. They can walk, in a small town. Give them lists of things like cookies, bananas, apples, candy, jello, aluminum foil, soda, baking powder, salad dressing mixes, band aids, kool aids, kleenex, cake mixes. Alert the Women in the Church to be ready to supply these things when the children come to their houses. Tell the children to go only to the homes of members of the congregation, but they are not to know the ladies are prepared for their coming. When they return to the church, have a big box ready to be packed to send to one of the missionaries your church supports, and use the cookies and fruit for refreshments for the children! Give three chocolate covered peanuts to each member of each team that brought in everything on their list. During refreshment time, read a letter from the missionary to whom they are sending their supplies, and wrap and address the box at the party to be sent immediately. You may let the children write letters telling the missionaries their fun in collecting the supplies, and asking them to write additional needs that the children could send to them.

A PROGRESSIVE SUPPER

Ask for volunteers from the congregation to serve courses of a progressive supper, and let the children ride bicycles from one house to another. The courses can include: hors d'oeuvres; chips and juice; salad and crackers; spaghetti and french bread; dessert; candy and nuts. At the last house have a time of singing around the piano, and close with a devotional.

A FELLOWSHIP SUPPER

Have the children invite their parents to a supper at the church. Plan a time of singing fun choruses and rounds. Follow this with skits by the children, dramatizing Bible stories.

Example: Have one child come out in pompous manner, followed by another with towel over arm. First sits on floor and pantomimes taking a bath. He then gets up and dries himself with towel handed him by the second child. He then takes another bath while the second child holds the towel. He dries off again. This is repeated seven times. Of course the crowd guesses that this is

Naaman in the Jordan River.

This can be followed by the children teaching the adults to play and participate in some of their supportive games.

Close the evening of fellowship and fun with a devotional by one of the fathers.

PINIATA BAG

A piniata bag can be successfully incorporated into most of the above-mentioned parties. Fill a paper mache balloon with tootsie rolls and bubble gum, around each of which has been pinned or taped a slip of paper containing a catechism question or Bible reference. When the bag is broken by the blindfolded person swinging the stick, and all the candy and gum fall out, have the teachers lined up at one end of the room, for no child can eat his candy or chew his gum until he's recited the verse or catechism answer pinned to it. Of course the children will grab as much as they can, but must say the required memory work before eating or chewing it!

The important thing is that each party and each game and each activity of catechism class is built around Scripture, and Christians having a good time in a clean, wholesome, enjoyable environment.

APPENDIX I

CONTESTS AND QUIZZES

It is good to have some quizzes on hand. The church library should contain one or more good game or church recreation books for your use. Some of the following have been picked up from various sources; others I have made. You can think of more, or have the Youth Fellowship make some for you.

These are good to have at parties. When the first guests arrive, give them a quiz and pen, and let them begin working while waiting for the festivities to start. Do this with the catechism children sometimes at their meetings. They'll enjoy working on some of the simpler ones in the winter while waiting for the program to start.

Whole parties can be built around several of them. Divide your group into several teams of five or six or more to a team, and let them work together on the quizzes, competing with the other teams.

Some of the quizzes are made for older children or adults. This was done in order to have something to appeal to older guests. They are fun to use at church fellowship suppers. The church that plays together has more fun!

Some are given merely for ideas for you to adapt to yor age group.

The young children love the **FIND THE BOOKS** puzzle. They can match hearts if the more difficult couples are omitted. The quiz entitled **FAMOUS PEOPLE YOU SHOULD KNOW** is given to you as an example of what you can do with the names of people in your own congregation. It will be popular and successful to play at almost any church function. **THE BIBLE FEAST** is more fun when done in groups. One variation of **NUMBER, PLEASE** is to reproduce it on a chalk board or large poster board, and let individuals from the crowd call out answers as the whole group works through it together. All the questions wouldn't have to be used each time — just enough to have fun. The participants are allowed and encouraged to use their Bibles with that one, but no references were given purposely, to require the participants to **FIND** the story without help.

After you've worked with catechumen awhile, I'm sure you'll find many more ways to liven up the program and keep the children interested. Remember that you are preparing children of today for a world of tomorrow. Study to show **THYSELF** approved unto God, a workman that needeth not to be ashamed, rightly dividing the word of truth unto these little ones. And may God bless you!

BIBLE CHARACTERS

1. A word that rhymes with aid and begins with same letter, a cheer, and a favorite portion of meat from the hog

2. A good winter dish or a country in South America, and short for upon

3. A day's work for a hen, and a man's name, or a beautiful yard

4. A short word meaning to tease, a second person pronoun, and a letter denoting singularity

5. The first two syllables are a descriptive word for silly or flighty, and the last is preposition for "on top of"

7. What a woman is likely to say if she sees a mouse, and a rap at the door

8. A one syllable expression of merriment, and two syllables that rhyme with and make you think of tobacco

9. A slang name for German soldiers in the war; a word expressing first-person ownership, and a sigh

10. An entrance into a house, and slang for curse

11. The top to a container, and the last part of a word for a bright thought

12. The sun, an exclamation, and the opposite of woman

13. An exclamation rhyming with tree, an instrument used in gardening, a letter denoting singularity, and the singular of have in the second-person

14. First letter of alphabet, where Goldilocks wound up, joint of the leg, word meaning "to leave or travel"

15. A colloquial negative answer, and a tune emitted from the mouth without words

16. A word meaning "not at all difficult," and to destroy life

17. Where most Christians would not stop after work, what a horse says, and public transportation

18. Two words put together meaning "transportation that belongs to me"

Answers to BIBLE CHARACTERS

1. Abraham
2. Chilion
3. Eglon
4. Joshua
5. Gideon
6. Noah
7. Enoch
8. Habakkuk
9. Jeremiah

10. Dorcas
11. Lydia
12. Solomon
13. Jehoahaz
14. Abednego
15. Nahum
16. Ezekiel
17. Barnabas
18. Micah

FAMOUS PEOPLE YOU SHOULD KNOW

1. Short for the carpenter; and catcher's equipment, and to cool.

   Joe Mitchell
   _____

2. Biblical response to a borrower, and first letter of alphabet; and male offspring of writer of Revelation.

   Linda Johnson
   _____

3. A flower in infancy; a user of a hoe, and a heavy weight.

   Bud Horton
   _____

4 65th book of Bible, your query if you didn't quite hear; and what you ask for if you haven't enough.

   Judy Moore
   _____

5. Not tight, and to behold; and the occupation of the two men on the cross, and a child that isn't a girl.

   Lucy Robinson
   _____

6. A Christmas Song; and a man that shoes horses.

   Carol Smith
   _____

7. Nickname for Eli's protege; and the ownership of the disciple who asked Christ to show us the father and it sufficeth us.

   Sam Phillips
   _____

8. The brother of John Thunder; and what Jesus implied that John the Baptist was not.

   James Reed
   _____

9. To duck for apples; and what will announce the second coming of Christ.

   Bob Horn
   _____

10. Short for the writer of the book between Hebrews and I Peter; and not old.

Jim Young

11. Verily; and what belongs to the first man.

Shirley Adams

12. To throw away; how John and Peter got to the empty tomb, and a little girl's toy.

Chuck Randal

13. To tap with light soft strokes; and a proper attitude for prayer.

Pat Neal

14. The first missionary and the sixth musical note; and the male child of a guy whose name rhymes with another word for daddy.

Paula Dawson

15. The happiest; and what the king does to the furnace to make it seven times hotter than it ought to be.

Gladys Stokes

16. Joseph's wife; and a color.

Mary Brown

17. The fisherman Jesus loved; and an old English word for the chairman of the session.

John Clark

18. Short for the doubter; and a temporary parent.

Tom Foster

-THIS IS A TIMED TEST-
-YOU HAVE ONLY FIVE MINUTES-
-WAIT FOR THE SIGNAL-

1. Read everything carefully before doing anything.
2. Put your name in the upper right hand corner of this page.
3. Circle the word NAME in sentence two.
4. Draw five small squares in the upper left hand corner.
5. Put a circle around each square.
6. Put an "X" in each square.
7. Sign your name under the title of this paper.
8. After the title write "YES, YES, YES."
9. Put an "X" in the lower left corner of this paper.
10. Put a circle completely around sentence in number seven.
11. Draw a triangle around the "X" you just put down.
12. On the back of this paper, multiply 703 x 66.
13. Draw a rectangle around the word "corner" in sentence four.
14. Loudly call out your first name when you get this far along.
15. If you think you have followed directions carefully to this point, call out "I HAVE."
16. On the reverse side of this paper add 8,950 and 9,805.
17. Put a CIRCLE around your answer and a square around the circle.
19. Punch three small holes in the top of this paper with your pencil point.
20. If you are the first person to reach this point, loudly call out, "I'M THE FIRST PERSON TO REACH THIS POINT AND AM THE LEADER IN THIS TEST."
21. Underline all even numbers on the left side of this paper.
22. Put a square around each written-out number on this page.
23. Loudly call out "I AM NEARLY FINISHED - I HAVE FOLLOWED INSTRUCTIONS."
24. Now that you have finished reading everything carefully, do only sentences one and two.

FIND THE BOOKS

While motoring in Palestine I saw Chief Mojud gesticulating wildly. His fez, raiment, and features were odd. I never saw so dismal a chief. On market days he pumps alms from everyone, a most common practice. A glance shows that he acts queerly. Excuse my speaking so, but he was showing a crowd how they used to revel at Ionian bouts, when the brew seemed good.

A fakir was seated on a hummock, minus hose and shirt, and wearing as comic a hat as they make. He pointed up eternally toward a rudely carved letter J on a high cliff. My companion excitedly cried, "See that J, oh, now I know we are near the ancient Ai. Was this Ai a holy place?"

From answers given elsewhere I'd say not. We asked the age of the big stone J. "O, eleven centuries at least." I knew that in such a jam escort was necessary; besides, our car was stuck in a rut here. So leaving the sedan, I elbowed nearer the fakir. A toothless hag gained access to his side, and she paused to rest herself. She hinted, "You have treasure?" To which I retorted, "Not I; moth, you know, and rust corrupt earthly store."

Mojud expressed a wish to accompany us, but I retorted, "Thy party we will not annex, O dusky chief. I am at the work of tracing a cargo of lost tobacco. That's my job." To the chief's expression of sorrow over the tobacco loss I answered, "It would all have gone up in smoke anyway."

My brother is a tramp (rover) B.S. from Harvard. His name is Eugene. Sister is nursing him now. They asked, "Where is the prodigal at?" I answered that it used to be correct to use it that way, but that the flu kept Eugene at home this year.

It's too bad. I ahm a homebody, roaming the Orient, and he is at home in bed.

Genesis	Esther	Joel	Haggai	John	Titus
Exodus	Job	Amos	Malachi	Acts	Hebrews
Judges	Psalms	Isaiah		Romans	James
Ruth	Proverbs	Obadiah	Matthew	Galatians	Peter
Kings	Daniel	Jonah	Mark	Colossians	Jude
Ezra	Hosea	Micah	Luke	Timothy	Revelation

FIND THE BOOKS
(Answers)

While motoring in Palestine I saw Chief Mo*jud ges*ticulating wildly. His *fez, rai*ment, and features were odd. I never saw so dis*mal a chi*ef. On *Mark*et days he pum*ps alms* from everyone, *a most* common practice. A glance shows that he *acts* queerly. Excuse my spea*king so*, but he was showing a crowd how they used to *revel at Ioni*an bouts, when *the brew* seemed good.

A fakir was seated on a hummock, minus *hose a*nd shirt, and wearing as co*mic a h*at as they make. He pointed u*p eter*nally toward a rudely carved letter *J on a h*igh cliff. My companion excitedly cried, "See that *J, oh, n*ow I know we are near the ancient Ai. Was th*is Ai a h*oly place?"

F*rom ans*wers given elsewhere I'd say not. We asked the age of the big stone *J*. "*O, el*even centuries at least." I knew that in such a *jam es*cort was necessary; besides, our car was stuck in a *rut h*ere. So leaving the se*dan, I el*bowed nearer the fakir. A toothless *hag gai*ned access to his side, and she paused to r*est her*self. She hinted, "You have treasure?" To which I retorted, "No*t I; moth, y*ou know, and rust corrupt earthly store."

Mo*jud e*xpressed a wish to accompany us, but I retorted, "Thy party we will not ann*ex, O dus*ky chief." I a*m at the w*ork of tracing a cargo of lost tobacco. "That's my *job*." To the chief's expression of sorrow over the toba*cco loss I ans*wered, "It would all have gone up in smoke anyway."

My brother is a tram*p (rover) B.S.* from Harvard. His name is Eu*gene. Sis*ter is nursing him now. They asked, "Where is the prod*igal at?" I ans*wered th*at it us*ed to be correct to use it that way, but that the *flu ke*pt Eugene at home this year.

It's to*o bad, I ah*m a homebody, roaming the Orient, and he is at home in bed.

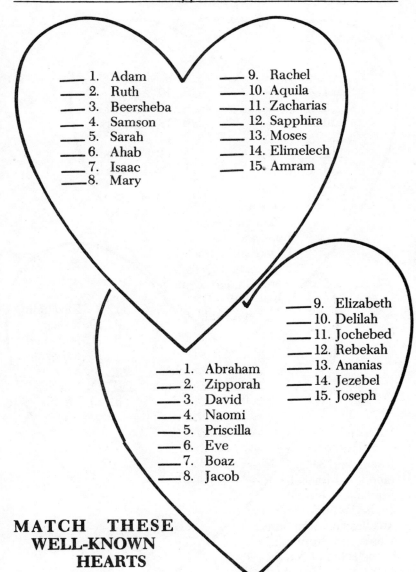

1. Adam
2. Ruth
3. Beersheba
4. Samson
5. Sarah
6. Ahab
7. Isaac
8. Mary

9. Rachel
10. Aquila
11. Zacharias
12. Sapphira
13. Moses
14. Elimelech
15. Amram

9. Elizabeth
10. Delilah
11. Jochebed
12. Rebekah
13. Ananias
14. Jezebel
15. Joseph

1. Abraham
2. Zipporah
3. David
4. Naomi
5. Priscilla
6. Eve
7. Boaz
8. Jacob

**MATCH THESE
WELL-KNOWN
HEARTS**

(Answers)

___6___ 1. Adam
___7___ 2. Ruth
___3___ 3. Beersheba
___10___ 4. Samson
___1___ 5. Sarah
___14___ 6. Ahab
___12___ 7. Isaac
___15___ 8. Mary

___8___ 9. Rachel
___5___ 10. Aquila
___9___ 11. Zacharias
___13___ 12. Sapphira
___2___ 13. Moses
___4___ 14. Elimelech
___11___ 15. Amram

Answers:
Adam and Eve
Boaz and Ruth
David and Bathsheba
Samson and Delilah
Abraham and Sarah
Isaac and
    Rebekah

___11___ 9. Elizabeth
___4___ 10. Delilah
___15___ 11. Jochebed
___7___ 12. Rebekah
___12___ 13. Ananias
___6___ 14. Jezebel
___8___ 15. Joseph

___5___ 1. Abraham
___13___ 2. Zipporah
___3___ 3. David
___14___ 4. Naomi
___10___ 5. Priscilla
___1___ 6. Eve
___2___ 7. Boaz
___9___ 8. Jacob

Ahab and
    Jezebel
Joseph and Mary
Jacob and Rachel
Aquila and Priscilla
Zacharias and Elizabeth
Ananias and Sapphira
Moses and Zipporah
Elimelech and Naomi
Amram and Jochebed

NUMBER PLEASE

1. Millenium x horsemen in Revelation ___

2. Days Christ in grave + Peter's denials ___

3. Years of wilderness wanderings x cubit length of Noah's ark ___

4. Lean years in Pharoah's dream x commandments ___

5. Sayings on cross + Pentateuch books ___

6. Days of rain during flood + lepers healed ___

7. Books written by Luke + O.T. books of poetry ___

8. Basketfuls left after feeding 5000 + tribes of Israel ___

9. Days Noah was in ark - age of Enoch when he died ___

10. Barley loaves that fed 5000 + persons in Godhead ___

11. Minor prophets - books written by John ___

___a. Days from Passover to Pentecost

___b. Apostles

___c. John's record of number of fishes caught in net

___d. Years of Israelite captivity in Egypt

___e. People saved in Noah's ark

___f. Basketfuls left after feeding 4000

___g. Job's children divided into two sets of ———

___h. Joshua's army marched around Jericho

___i. Years Israelites slaves to Babylon

___j. Boards in back end of tabernacle

___k. Longest Psalm

12. Sent out by Christ in twos+ deacons in early church

13. Books of O.T. + number of Gods

14. N.T. books + cherubim wings

15. Philistines killed by Shamgar's ox goad + books in Bible

16. Sheep safely in fold in parable + boards in each side of tabernacle

17. Kinds of soil in parable of sower + living creatures in Ezekiel's vision

18. Men in Gideon's final army + cubit length of tabernacle court

19. Days God rested + major prophet books

20. Days spies were in Canaan x gifts brought by wise men

21. Times Naaman bathed in Jordan - spies that said Canaan could be taken

___l. Saved from each tribe of Jews in Revelation

___m. Pauline Epistles

___n. Elders about throne in Revelation

___o. Christ fed with 7 loaves and few fishes

___p. Philistines Samson killed with jawbone of an ass

___q. Tribes in northern kingdom

___r. Days Christ tempted in wilderness

___s. Number of the Revelation beast

___t. Traditional age of Christ at death

___u. Commandment to honor parents

22. Days work required in 4th commandment + Asian churches in Revelation ___|

___v. Petitions in Lord's prayer

23. Chapters in Proverbs - pieces of silver Judas received ___|

___w. Days God worked in creation

24. Age of Christ when lost in temple ___

___x. Stones it took to kill Goliath

25. Fed with 5 barley loaves, 2 fishes –+– rocks David picked from stream ___

___y. Approximate number of disciples in upper room at Pentecost

26. 5000 to be fed seated in companies of____, + lost sheep in parable, x men thrown into fiery furnace ___|

___z. Number of loaves of shewbread

NUMBER PLEASE
(Answers)

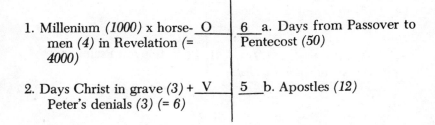

1. Millenium *(1000)* x horse- men *(4)* in Revelation *(= 4000)*   O ___|

___6___ a. Days from Passover to Pentecost *(50)*

2. Days Christ in grave *(3)* + Peter's denials *(3) (= 6)*   V ___|

___5___ b. Apostles *(12)*

3. Years of wilderness wand- L
erings *(40)* x cubit length
(300) of Noah's ark(=
12000)

26 c. John's record of number
of fishes caught in net *(153)*

4. Lean years in Pharoah's I
dream *(7)* x command-
ments *(10)* *(= 70)*

18 d. Years of Israelite captivity in Egypt *(400)*

5. Sayings on cross *(7)* + B
Pentateuch books*(5)* *(=*
12)

10 e. People saved in Noah's
ark *(8)*

6. Days of rain during flood A
(40) + lepers healed *(10)*
(= 50)

7 f. Basketfuls left after
feeding 4000 *(7)*

7. Books written by Luke *(2)* F
+ O.T. books of poetry
(5) *(= 7)*

12 g. Job's children divided
into two sets of_____*(10)*

8. Basketfuls left after feed- N
ing 5000 *(12)* + tribes of
Israel *(12)* *(= 24)*

11 h. Joshua's army marched
around Jericho *(7)*

9. Days Noah was in ark *(375)* Q
- age of Enoch when he
died *(365)* *(= 10)*

4 i. Years Israelites slaves to
Babylon *(70)*

10. Barley loaves that fed 5000 E
(5) + persons in Godhead
(3) *(= 8)*

17 j. Boards in back end of
tabernacle *(8)*

11. Minor prophets *(12)* - H
books written by John
(5) *(= 7)*

16 k. Longest Psalm *(119)*

12. Sent out by Christ in twos (70)÷deacons (7) in early church (= 10) G

3 l. Saved from each tribe of Jews in Revelation (12000)

13. Books of O.T. (39) + number of Gods (1) (= 40) R

22 m. Pauline Epistles (13)

14. N.T. books (27) + cherubim wings (6) (= 33) T

8 n. Elders about throne in Heaven (24)

15. Philistines killed by Shamgar's ox goad (600) + books in Bible (66) (= 666) S

1 o. Christ fed with 7 loaves and few fishes (4000)

16. Sheep safely in fold in parable (99) + boards in each side of tabernacle (20) (= 119) K

25 p. Philistines Samson killed with jawbone of an ass (1000)

17. Kinds of soil in parable of sower (4) + living creatures in Ezekiel's vision (4) (= 8) I

9 q. Tribes in northern kingdom (10)

18. Men in Gideon's final army (300) + cubit length of tabernacle court (100) (= 400) D

13 r. Days Christ tempted in wilderness (40)

19. Days God rested (1) + major prophet books (5) (= 6) W

15 s. Number of the Revelation beast (666)

20. Days spies were in Canaan (40) x gifts brought by wise men (3) (= 120) __Y__

14 t. Traditional age of Christ at death (33)

1. Times Naaman bathed in Jordan (7) - spies that said Canaan could be taken (2) (= 5) __U__

21 u. Commandment to honor parents (5)

22. Days work required in 4th commandment (6) + Asian churches in Revelation (7) (= 13) __M__

2 v. Petitions in Lord's prayer (6)

23. Chapters in Proverbs (31) - pieces of silver Judas received (30) (= 1) __X__

19 w. Days God worked in creation (6)

24. Age of Christ when lost in temple (12) __Z__

23. x. Stones it took to kill Goliath (1)

25. Fed with 5 barley loaves, 2 fishes (5000) ÷ rocks David picked from stream (5) (= 1000) __P__

20 y. Approximate number of disciples in upper room at Pentecost (120)

26. 5000 to be fed seated in companies of_____(50) + lost sheep in parable (1), x men thrown into fiery furnace (3) (= 153) __C__

24 z. Number of loaves of shewbread (12)

A BIBLICAL FEAST

Served by Harmat _____
(Who else!)

EQUIPMENT:
blate _____
cholt _____
kannip _____
hessid _____
lowbs _____
tripech _____
puc _____
oponss _____
finek _____
rilves _____
kfro _____

DECOR:
skadilcentc _____
ladcens _____
woslerf _____

MENU:
Hors d'oeuvres:
tramnigesope (red, scarce, delightful) _____
vilose (green, and black) _____
plapse (good, in the eye or in pictures) _____
tloscus (well, one person liked 'em!) _____

Salad:
clarig (it'll make you strong) _____
skele (they keep plumbers in business) _____
osionn (you'll cry) _____
brusmcecu (good for complexion & blood pressure) _____
lio (mechanics love it) _____
lemons (the bigger the better) _____
Entre buffet:
   team (or greet) _____
   laqui (to shrink, fade, or wither) _____
   balm (and mint jelly, of course) _____
   dik (just funning) _____
   flac (the prodigal ate cholesterol) _____
   hifs (I just love to) _____
   taog (best barbequed) _____
   gips (how do Jews eat eggs without it? _____
drabe (the crutch of sustenance) _____
breyal (pearl herself) _____
twahe (a shock) _____
norc (not for snaggled tooth chillun) _____
Beverage:
trawe (goes well with soap) _____
niwe (get barefooted to make) _____
kilm (I can't do it but I can sure drink it) _____
Dessert:
yohen (sweetheart) _____
heyon bomc (don't use it to fix your hair) _____
sriansi (makes me think of fruit cake) _____
sgif (good for boils and newtons) _____
trifu (every kind is delicious) _____
wons (makes good ice cream) _____
sheeec (smile when you say it) _____
praegs (good even when trampled upon) _____

PREPARATION:
lobri _____
charped _____

dankeed _____

leobid _____

coko _____

shetee _____

A BIBLICAL FEAST
(Answers)

Served by Harmat __*Martha*__

(Who else!)

EQUIPMENT:

blate _____ *table*

cholt _____ *cloth*

kannip _____ *napkin*

hessid _____ *dishes*

lowbs _____ *bowls*

tripech _____ *pitcher*

puc _____ *cup*

oponss _____ *spoons*

finek _____ *knife*

rilves _____ *silver*

kfro _____ *fork*

DECOR:

skadilcentc _____ *candlestick*

ladcens _____ *candles*

woslerf _____ *flowers*

MENU:

Hors d'oeuvres:

tramnigesope (red, scarce, delightful) __*pomegranates*__

vilose (green, and black) _____ *olives*

plapse (good, in the eye or in pictures)__*apples*__

tloscus (well, one person liked 'em!) __*locusts*__

Salad:
clarig (it'll make you strong) ____ *garlic*
skele (they keep plumbers in business) __ *leeks*
osionn (you'll cry) ____ *onions*
brusmcecu (good for complexion & blood pressure) *cucumbers*
lio (mechanics love it) ____ *oil*
lemons (the bigger the better) ____ *melons*
Entre buffet:
  team (or greet) ____ *meat*
  laqui (to shrink, fade, or wither) ____ *quail*
  balm (and mint jelly, of course) ____ *lamb*
  dik (just funning) ____ *kid*
  flac (the prodigal ate cholesterol) ____ *calf*
  hifs (I just love to) ____ *fish*
  taog (best barbequed) ____ *goat*
  gips (how do Jews eat eggs without it? *pigs*
drabe (the crutch of sustenance) ____ *bread*
breyal (pearl herself) ____ *barley*
twahe (a shock) ____ *wheat*
norc (not for snaggled tooth chillun) ____ *corn*
Beverage:
trawe (goes well with soap) ____ *water*
niwe (get barefooted to make) ____ *wine*
kilm (I can't do it but I can sure drink it) __ *milk*
Dessert:
yohen (sweetheart) ____ *honey*
heyon bomc (don't use it to fix your hair) *honey comb*
sriansi (makes me think of fruit cake) ____ *raisins*
sgif (good for boils and newtons) ____ *figs*
trifu (every kind is delicious) ____ *fruit*
wons (makes good ice cream) ____ *snow*
sheeec (smile when you say it) ____ *cheese*
praegs (good even when trampled upon) *grapes*

PREPARATION:
lobri ____ *broil*
charped ____ *parched*

dankeed	*kneaded*
leobid	*boiled*
coko	*cook*
shetee	*seethe*

NOTES